StartUp

Ken Beatty, Series Consultant

HM Austin
Sharon Goldstein
Robin N. Longshaw
Kimberly Russell
Geneva Tesh

StartUp 3

Pearson, 221 River Street, Hoboken, NJ 07030

Staff credits: The people who made up the StartUp team representing editorial, production, and design are Pietro Alongi, Héctor González Álvarez, Gregory Bartz, Peter Benson, Magdalena Berkowska, Stephanie Callahan, Jennifer Castro, Tracey Munz Cataldo, Dave Dickey, Gina DiLillo, Irene Frankel, Sarah Henrich, Christopher Leonowicz, Bridget McLaughlin, Kamila Michalak, Laurie Neaman, Alison Pei, Jennifer Raspiller, Jeremy Schaar, Katherine Sullivan, Stephanie Thornton, Paula Van Ells, and Joseph Vella.

Cover credit: Front cover: Matteo Colombo/Getty Images. Back cover: Klaus Vedfelt/Getty Images (Level 1); Alexandre Moreau/Getty Images (Level 2); Matteo Colombo/Getty Images (Level 3); Javier Osores/EyeEm/Getty Images (Level 4); Liyao Xie/Getty Images (Level 5); Ezra Bailey/Getty Images (Level 6); guvendemir/Getty Images (Level 7); Yusuke Shimazu/EyeEm/Getty Images (Level 8); tovovan/Shutterstock (icons)

Text composition: emc design ltd

Library of Congress cataloging-in-publication data on file.

Photo and illustration credits: see pages 166–167

Printed in the United States of America

ISBN-10: 0-13-468416-8

ISBN-13: 978-0-13-468416-1

1 18

ISBN-10: 0-13-517844-4 (with app and Online Practice)

ISBN-13: 978-0-13-517844-7 (with app and Online Practice)

1 18

ACKNOWLEDGMENTS

We would like to thank the following people for their insightful and helpful comments and suggestions.

Maria Alam, Extension Program-Escuela Americana, San Salvador, El Salvador; **Milton Ascencio**, Universidad Don Bosco, Soyapango, El Salvador; **Raul Avalos**, CALUSAC, Guatemala City, Guatemala; **Adrian Barnes**, Instituto Chileno Norteericano, Santiago, Chile; **Laura Bello**, Centro de Idiomas Xalapa, Universidad Veracruzana, Xalapa, México; **Jeisson Alonso Rodriguez Bonces**, Fort Dorchester High School, Bogotá, Colombia; **Juan Pablo Calderón Bravo**, Manpower English, Santiago, Chile; **Ellen J. Campbell**, RMIT, Ho Chi Minh City, Vietnam; **Vinicio Cancinos**, CALUSAC, Guatemala City, Guatemala; **Viviana Castilla**, Centro de Enseñanza de Lenguas Extranjeras UN, México; **Bernal Cespedes**, ULACIT, Tournón, Costa Rica; **Carlos Celis**, Cel. Lep Idiomas S.A., São Paulo, Brazil; **Carlos Eduardo Aguilar Cortes**, Universidad de los Andes, Bogotá, Colombia; **Solange Lopes Vinagre Costa**, Senac-SP, São Paulo, Brazil; **Isabel Cubilla**, Panama Bilingüe, Panama City, Panama; **Victoria Dieste**, Alianza Cultural Uruguay-Estados Unidos, Montevideo, Uruguay; **Francisco Domerque**, Georgal Idiomas, México City, México; **Vern Eaton**, St. Giles International, Vancouver, Canada; **Maria Fajardo**, Extension Program-Escuela Americana, San Salvador, El Salvador; **Diana Elizabeth Leal Ffrench**, Let's Speak English, Cancún, México; **Rosario Giraldez**, Alianza Cultural Uruguay-Estados Unidos, Montevideo, Uruguay; **Lourdes Patricia Rodríguez Gómez**, Instituto Tecnológico de Chihuahua, Chihuahua, México; **Elva Elizabeth Martínez de González**, Extension Program-Escuela Americana, San Salvador, El Salvador; **Gabriela Guel**, Centro de Idiomas de la Normal Superior, Monterrey, México; **Ana Raquel Fiorani Horta**, SENAC, Ribeirão Preto, Brazil; **Carol Hutchinson**, Heartland International English School, Winnipeg, Canada; **Deyanira Solís Juárez**, Centro de Idiomas de la Normal Superior, Monterrey, México; **Miriam de Käppel**, Colegio Bilingüe El Prado, Guatemala City, Guatemala; **Ikuko Kashiwabara**, Osaka Electro-Communication University, Neyagawa, Japan; **Steve Kirk**, Nippon Medical School, Tokyo, Japan; **Jill Landry**, GEOS Languages Plus, Ottawa, Canada; **Tiffany MacDonald**, East Coast School of Languages, Halifax, Canada; **Angélica Chávez Escobar Martínez**, Universidad de León, León, Guanajuato, México; **Renata Martinez**, CALUSAC, Guatemala City, Guatemala; **Maria Alejandra Mora**, Keiser International Language Institute, San Marcos, Carazo, Nicaragua; **Alexander Chapetón Morales**, Abraham Lincoln School, Bogotá, Colombia; **José Luis Castro Moreno**, Universidad de León, León, Guanajuato, México; **Yukari Naganuma**, Eikyojuku for English Teachers, Tokyo, Japan; **Erina Ogawa**, Daito Bunka University, Tokyo, Japan; **Carolina Zepeda Ortega**, Let's Speak English, Cancún, México; **Lynn Passmore**, Vancouver International College, Vancouver, Canada; **Noelle Peach**, EC English, Vancouver, Canada; **Ana-Marija Petrunic,** George Brown College, Toronto, Canada; **Romina Planas**, Centro Cultural Paraguayo Americano, Asunción, Paraguay; **Sara Elizabeth Portela**, Centro Cultural Paraguayo Americano, Asunción, Paraguay; **Luz Rey**, Centro Colombo Americano, Bogotá, Colombia; **Ana Carolina González Ramírez**, Universidad de Costa Rica, San José, Costa Rica; **Octavio Garduno Ruiz**, AIPT Service S.C., Coyoacán, México; **Amado Sacalxot**, Colegio Lehnsen Americas, Guatemala City, Guatemala; **Deyvis Sanchez**, Instituto Cultural Dominico-Americano, Santo Domingo, Dominican Republic; **Lucy Slon**, JFK Adult Centre, Montreal, Canada; **Scott Stulberg**, University of Regina, Regina, Canada; **Maria Teresa Suarez**, Colegios APCE, San Salvador, El Salvador; **Daniel Valderrama**, Centro Colombo Americano, Bogotá, Colombia; **Kris Vicca**, Feng Chia University, Taichung, Taiwan; **Sairy Matos Villanueva**, Centro de Actualización del Magisterio, Chetumal, Q.R., México; **Edith Espino Villarreal**, Universidad Tecnológica de Panama, El Dorado, Panama; **Isabela Villas Boas**, Casa Thomas Jefferson, Brasília, Brazil

LEARNING OBJECTIVES

WELCOME UNIT
page 2   In the classroom | Learn about your book | Learn about your app

Unit	Vocabulary	Grammar	Conversation / Speaking	Listening
1 **What's going on with you?** **page 5**	• Activities • Life events • Tourist activities	• Present continuous for temporary situations • Simple past + *when, before,* and *after* • Suggestions with *Let's* and *Why don't*	• Talk about what you're doing • Talk about your family • Make and respond to invitations **Skill** Respond to a suggestion	
2 **What do you think?** **page 17**	• Sensory verbs • Attitudes • Adverbs of manner	• Sensory verbs + *like* • *Be* + adjective + infinitive • Adverbs of degree and manner	• Describe two similar things • Describe personal traits • Talk about how people do things **Skill** Express disagreement	• Listen to a podcast about feedback **Skill** Listen for paraphrasing
3 **How was your weekend?** **page 29**	• Participial adjectives • Past participles • Adjectives to describe feelings	• Participial adjectives • Present perfect for past experiences • Ability / Inability in the past	• Express how you feel • Talk about past activities • Describe your emotions **Skill** Change the topic	• Listen to a podcast of an unusual story **Skill** Listen for descriptions
4 **Would you like something to eat?** **page 41**	• Lunch foods • Partitives • Food at a barbecue	• Count and non-count nouns with *some, any,* and *no* • *Much / Many / A lot of* and *How much / How many* • *Enough* and *Too much / Too many* + nouns	• Talk about food choices • Talk about food customs • Talk about what you have and need **Skill** Hesitate	• Listen to a podcast about blue zones **Skill** Listen for comparisons
5 **When can we meet?** **page 53**	• Technology at work • Technology issues and hardware • Meeting preparation	• *Could* and *should* for suggestions • *Will, may,* and *might* to express likelihood • *Have to / Need to* for obligation and necessity	• Make and respond to suggestions • Identify problems and solutions • Talk about what you need to do **Skill** Show you understand	• Listen to phone messages about tech issues **Skill** Listen for instructions

Pronunciation	Reading	Writing	Media Project	Learning Strategy
• Main stress • Thought groups	• Read about work friendships **Skill** Find the topic	• Write an email to make plans **Skill** Use transition words for time	• Describe photos of activities you've been doing lately	**Grammar** • Learn grammar in phrases and sentences
• The letter *s* • Syllables and stress	• Read about life-changing advice **Skill** Find the main idea	• Write a recommendation **Skill** Write complete sentences in formal writing	• Make a video about a product that you like	**Vocabulary** • Describe what you see
• The *-ed* ending in adjectives • Stressed words	• Read about extreme sports **Skill** Notice text structure: Interviews	• Write a description of a trip **Skill** Use descriptive adjectives	• Describe photos of your weekend	**Pronunciation** • Flashcards for pronunciation
• Dropped syllables • Phrases with *of*	• Read about the science of dessert **Skill** Identify supporting details	• Write about a holiday meal **Skill** Add sentence variety	• Make a video about a dish you want to cook and what foods you need to make it	**Grammar** • Use grammar on flashcards
• Consonant groups • Weak and blended pronunciation of *to*	• Read about 3D printing **Skill** Identify text structure: Problem / Solution	• Write advice on how to manage your time **Skill** Use qualifiers	• Make a video about a technology that helps you	**Vocabulary** • Label a picture

Unit	Vocabulary	Grammar	Conversation / Speaking	Listening
6 **How's your lunch?** **page 65**	• Adjectives to describe food • Gift items • Storytelling expressions	• *Too* and *enough* + adjectives • Verbs + two objects • Past continuous; past continuous with *when*	• Talk about food preferences • Talk about gifts • Talk about past events **Skill** Show surprise	• Listen to a story about fate **Skill** Listen for intonation
7 **Where are you going?** **page 77**	• Verbs / Adjectives + prepositions • Words to describe a place • Geographical features	• Gerunds as objects of prepositions • *Would like / love / hate* + infinitive • Superlative adjectives	• Talk about an upcoming trip • Talk about what you would like to do • Talk about geographical features **Skill** End a conversation	• Listen to a quiz show about geography **Skill** Listen for specific information
8 **What are you doing tonight?** **page 89**	• Instruments and musicians • Evening events • Healthy habits	• Questions about the subject and object • *So / Because (of)* to show cause and effect • Time expressions	• Talk about music • Talk about evening plans • Describe habits and routines **Skill** Turn down an invitation politely	• Listen to a podcast about technology **Skill** Listen for examples and supporting statements
9 **Where do you want to meet?** **page 101**	• Living room furniture and decor • Reasons for being late • Places in and around the house	• Future with *will*, *be going to*, present continuous, and simple present • Indirect questions • Adverbs and adverbial phrases of place	• Talk about plans • Talk about reasons for being late • Talk about where things are **Skill** Ask if there is a problem	• Listen to a story about a cat **Skill** Predicting
10 **How long did you work there?** **page 113**	• Job interviews • Work experience • Soft skills	• Tag questions • Present perfect with *for* and *since*; *how long* and *ever* • Information questions with the present perfect	• Start a job interview • Talk about your work experience • Give more details about your work experience **Skill** Express an opinion	

Pronunciation	Reading	Writing	Media Project	Learning Strategy
• The vowels /i/ and /ɪ/ • Weak pronunciation of object pronouns	• Read about unique restaurants **Skill** Construct mental images	• Write about an unusual food **Skill** Show contrast	• Describe photos of a celebration	**Pronunciation** • Find new sources
• Blending: *want to* ("wanna") and *going to* ("gonna") • Dropping the /t/ and linking in superlatives	• Read about unusual hotels **Skill** Identify point of view	• Write a description of a place **Skill** Include one topic per paragraph	• Describe photos of a place	**Grammar** • Learn grammar in context
• Intonation: Showing enthusiasm • Main stress to emphasize a contrast	• Read about the power of music **Skill** Ask and answer questions	• Write suggestions for meeting people **Skill** Write informally	• Describe photos of your healthy habits	**Vocabulary** • Create connections
• The letter *a* • Stress in compounds	• Read product reviews **Skill** Identify fact vs. opinion	• Write about your dream home **Skill** Use parallel structure	• Make a video about a room you'd like to redecorate	**Pronunciation** • Practice word stress for pronunciation
• Stressed syllables in nouns • Weak and contracted pronunciations of *have* and *has*	• Read interview advice **Skill** Make associations	• Write a cover letter **Skill** Consider your audience	• Make a video about your dream job	**Grammar** • Tell a story to practice verb tenses

Key

▶ 00-00 audio   ▶ video   ActiveTeach

abc flashcards   ▶ COACH video/coach   🔍 web search

TO THE TEACHER

Welcome to StartUp

StartUp is an innovative eight-level, general American English course for adults and young adults who want to make their way in the world and need English to do it. The course takes students from CEFR A1 to C1 and enables teachers and students to track their progress in detail against the Global Scale of English (GSE) Learning Objectives.

StartUp Level	GSE Range	CEFR	Description
1	22-33	A1	Beginner
2	30-37	A2	High beginner
3	34-43	A2+	Low intermediate
4	41-51	B1	Intermediate

StartUp Level	GSE Range	CEFR	Description
5	49-58	B1+	High intermediate
6	56-66	B2	Upper intermediate
7	64-75	B2+	Low advanced
8	73-84	C1	Advanced

English for 21st century learners

StartUp helps your students develop the spoken and written language they need to communicate in their personal, academic, and work lives. In each lesson, you help students build the collaborative and critical thinking skills so essential for success in the 21st century. *StartUp* allows students to learn the language in ways that work for them: anytime anywhere. The Pearson Practice English App allows students to access their English practice on the on the go. Additionally, students have all the audio and video files at their fingertips in the app and on the Pearson English Portal.

Personalized, flexible teaching

The unit structure and the wealth of support materials give you options to personalize the class to best meet your students' needs. *StartUp* gives you the freedom to focus on different strands and skills; for example, you can spend more class time on listening and speaking. You can choose to teach traditionally or flip the learning. You can teach sections of the lesson in the order you prefer. And you can use the ideas in the Teacher's Edition to help you extend and differentiate instruction, particularly for mixed-ability and for large and small classes.

Motivating and relevant learning

StartUp creates an immersive learning experience with a rich blend of multimedia videos and interactive activities, including interactive flashcards for vocabulary practice; Grammar Coach and Pronunciation Coach videos; interactive grammar activities; podcasts, interviews, and other audio texts for listening practice; humorous, engaging videos with an international cast of characters for modeling conversations; high-interest video talks beginning at Level 5; media project videos in Levels 1–4 and presentation skills videos in Levels 5–8 for end-of-unit skills consolidation.

Access at your fingertips

StartUp provides students with everything they need to extend their learning to their mobile device. The app empowers students to take charge of their learning outside of class, allowing them to practice English whenever and wherever they want, online or offline. The app provides practice of vocabulary, grammar, listening, and conversation. Students can go to any lesson by scanning a QR code on their Student Book page or through the app menu. The app also provides students with access to all the audio and video files from the course.

Components

For the Teacher

StartUp provides everything you need to plan, teach, monitor progress, and assess learning.

The *StartUp* **ActiveTeach** front-of-class tool allows you to

- zoom in on the page to focus the class's attention
- launch the vocabulary flashcard decks from the page
- use tools, like a highlighter, to emphasize specific text
- play all the audio texts and videos from the page
- pop up interactive grammar activities
- move easily to and from any cross-referenced pages

The interleaved **Teacher's Edition** includes

- an access code to the Pearson Practice English App and all digital resources
- language and culture notes
- teaching tips to help you improve your teaching practice
- *look for* notes to help assess students' performance
- answer keys to all Student Book exercises on the facing page of the notes
- and more!

Teacher's Digital Resources, all available on the Pearson English Portal, include

- Teacher Methodology Handbook
- A unit walkthrough
- ActiveTeach front-of-class software
- ExamView assessment software
- Teacher's notes for every Student Book page
- Rubrics for speaking and writing
- Hundreds of reproducible worksheets
- Answer keys for all practice
- Audio and video scripts
- The GSE Teacher Mapping Booklet
- The GSE Toolkit

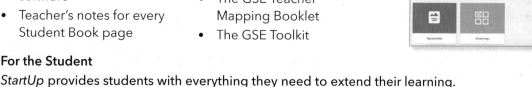

For the Student

StartUp provides students with everything they need to extend their learning.

The optional **MyEnglishLab for *StartUp*** gives students more formal online practice and provides immediate feedback, hints, and tips. It includes

- grammar practice with remedial activities and access to all the Grammar Coach videos
- vocabulary practice, including games and flashcards
- speaking and pronunciation activities, including access to all the conversation videos and Pronunciation Coach videos
- listen-and-record practice that lets students record themselves and compare their recordings to models
- auto-graded reading and writing practice that reinforces skills taught in the Student Book
- summative assessments that measure students' mastery of listening, vocabulary, grammar, pronunciation, and reading
- a gradebook, which records scores on practice and assessments, that both students and you can use to help monitor progress and plan further practice

The optional *StartUp* **Workbook** provides practice of vocabulary, grammar, reading, and writing and includes self-assessments of grammar and vocabulary.

WELCOME UNIT

1 IN THE CLASSROOM

A Get to know your classmates

Play the Name Game.

B Ask for help

▶ 00-01 **Complete the conversations with sentences from the box. Then listen and check your answers.**

~~Could you explain that?~~	I'm sorry. What page?
Did you say a pen?	What's the word for this in English?
Do you mean first we should work alone?	What I mean is you shouldn't read aloud.

C ROLE PLAY Choose a conversation from 1B. Make your own conversation. Use different information.

2 LEARN ABOUT YOUR BOOK

1. Look at pages iv–vii. What information is on those pages?

   _____

2. How many units are in the book? _____

3. How many lessons are in each unit? _____

4. Where is the grammar practice? _____

5. Look at the QR code [QR]. Find the icon on page 7. What does it mean? _____

   _____

6. Look at the ☐ I CAN STATEMENT at the bottom of page 7. What does it tell you? _____

   _____

7. Look at this icon 🔍. Find it on page 13. What does it mean?

   _____

3 LEARN ABOUT YOUR APP

1. Look inside the front cover. Where can you go to download the Pearson Practice English App for StartUp? _____

2. Where are the instructions for registering for the app? _____

   _____

3. Look at the picture of the app. What do you see?

   _____

4. Look at the picture again. Fill in the blanks with the numbers 1–3.
   a. Number _____ shows the practice activities.
   b. Number _____ shows the video files.
   c. Number _____ shows the audio files.

5. Look at the picture again. What does this ☁ mean? _____

6. Look at the QR code on page 7 again. What happens when you scan the code? _____

   _____

TSW MEDIA
MEET THE PEOPLE OF TSW MEDIA

TSW Media is a big company with big ideas. It has offices all over the world. It works with international clients to help them market their products and services.

MARIO CALVO
Promotions manager

▶ 00-02 Hi! My name is Mario Calvo. I'm from Ecuador. I work in the Quito office and I'm a promotions manager. I'm married—my wife and I are going to have a baby very soon.

SARAH GOLD
Head of events planning

▶ 00-05 Hey there! My name is Sarah Gold. I work in the Toronto, Canada office. I'm the head of events planning. I'm married, with one son. My hobby is running triathlons.

LUCAS MORALES
Illustrator

▶ 00-03 Hi! I'm Lucas Morales. I'm from San José, Costa Rica. I'm an illustrator. I love comic books and my favorite movies and TV shows are science fiction and fantasy.

ALBA PARDO
Accounts manager

▶ 00-06 Hello. My name is Alba Pardo. I am an accounts manager and I work in Mexico City. I live with my two children and my mother. My office is full of plants and flowers.

ERIC PARK
Copywriter

▶ 00-04 Hello. I'm Eric Park and I'm from Seoul, South Korea. I'm a copywriter. I love riding my bicycle, and I've ridden my bike across Korea a few times.

MANDY WILSON
Market researcher

▶ 00-07 Hi! I'm Mandy Wilson and I'm from New York City. I'm a market researcher. I live with my sister and we have a cat. I love to knit and right now, I'm knitting my boyfriend another scarf. He's a firefighter.

1 WHAT'S GOING ON WITH YOU?

LEARNING GOALS

In this unit, you
- ⊘ talk about what you're doing
- ⊘ talk about your family
- ⊘ make and respond to invitations
- ⊘ read about work friendships
- ⊘ write an email to make plans

GET STARTED

A Read the unit title and learning goals.

B Look at the photo of colleagues talking. What do you see?

SARAH GOLD
@SarahG

I'm at our main office for a week. Looking forward to meeting colleagues from all over the world!

C Now read Sarah's message. What is she doing this week?

SARAH GOLD
@SarahG

Can't wait to see my good friend and co-worker Mario. I wonder what's new with him.

 1 VOCABULARY Activities

A ▶01-01 **Listen. Then listen and repeat.**

take — an online class | guitar lessons

study — Japanese

graphic design

look for — an apartment

a job

spend time with — family | friends

work at — a restaurant

a hospital

play — tennis

chess

B Look at the verbs and activities in 1A. List one more activity for each verb.   *take piano lessons*

C PAIRS Are you familiar with any of the activities in 1A or something similar? Discuss.

2 GRAMMAR Present continuous for temporary situations

Affirmative statements			Negative statements			
Subject	*Be*	Verb + *-ing*	Subject	*Be*	*Not*	Verb + *-ing*
I	am		I	am		
He	is	**taking** a class.	He	is	not	**looking** for a job anymore.
They	are		They	are		

Use contractions, such as *I'm, he's, she's*, etc., in spoken English and informal writing.

Yes / No question			Short answers	
Be	Subject	Verb + *-ing*	Affirmative	Negative
Are	you	still **living** in Quito?	Yes, I **am**.	No, I**'m not**.

Information questions				Answers		
Wh- word	*Be*	Subject	Verb + *-ing*	Subject	*Be*	Verb + *-ing*
What	is	Mario	**doing** these days?	He	is	**taking** a class.
Where	are	they	**studying** now?	They	are	**studying** in the office.

Notes
- Use *these days* for a situation that is temporary. *I am traveling a lot **these days***.
- Use *still* for a situation that continues to be true. *Mario is **still** living in Quito*.
- Use *not…anymore* for a situation that is no longer true. *He is **not** living in Atlanta **anymore***.

>> FOR PRACTICE, GO TO PAGE 125

3 PRONUNCIATION

A ▶01-03 Listen. Notice the main stress. Then listen and repeat.

A: What are you **doing** these days?

B: I'm taking an online **class**. What about **you**?

A: Well, I'm living in New **York** now.

B ▶01-04 Listen. Underline the word that has the main stress in each sentence. Then listen and repeat.

1. A: What's going on with you?
   B: Well, I'm taking tennis lessons.
2. A: What's your sister doing?
   B: She's working at a bank now.

3. A: Is your brother still living in Madrid?
   B: Yes, but he's moving to Toronto soon.

C PAIRS Practice the conversations in 3B.

4 CONVERSATION

A ▶01-05 Listen or watch. Circle the correct answers.

1. Mario is looking for a new house because ___ .
   a. his wife is going to have a baby
   b. he's moving to a new city
   c. he's going to school
2. Mario is learning about ___ .
   a. computer software
   b. photography
   c. engineering

3. Sarah is taking ___ in the spring.
   a. a workshop
   b. a class
   c. a vacation

B ▶01-06 Listen or watch. Complete the conversation.

Sarah: So, what are you doing these days?

Mario: I'm taking an online class.

Sarah: That's _____ .

Mario: Yeah, it's pretty interesting. What's going on with you?

Sarah: Well, I'm studying Japanese.

Mario: That's really _____ !

C ▶01-07 Listen and repeat. Then practice with a partner.

D PAIRS Make new conversations. Use these words or your own ideas.

studying graphic design
taking guitar lessons

5 TRY IT YOURSELF

A PAIRS Talk about what you're doing these days. Ask your partner questions.

B WALK AROUND Ask your classmates what they're doing these days. Report to the class. Is there someone who is doing the same thing as you?

■ I CAN TALK ABOUT WHAT I'M DOING.

SARAH GOLD

@SarahG

Having a great time at the conference. I'm learning so much about my co-workers.

 1 VOCABULARY Life events

A ▶01-08 Listen. Then listen and repeat.

 lose a job

 quit a job

 start a business

 get engaged

 graduate from college

 apply to graduate school

 change careers

 adopt a pet

 have a baby

 get a certificate

B Look at the life events in 1A. Put the events into the groups below.

School	Career	Personal
	lose a job	

C PAIRS Tell your partner about three things from 1A that you or a family member has done.

 2 GRAMMAR Simple past + *when*, *before*, and *after*

COACH

Use *when, before,* and *after* to introduce a time clause. Use *when* or *after* to introduce the action that happened first. Use *before* to introduce the action that happened second.

Affirmative statements

Main clause	Past time clause
They **moved** to a new house	**when** they **had** a baby. *(They had a baby first.)*
He **took** some classes	**before** he **opened** the café. *(He opened the café second.)*
She **went** to Kyoto	**after** she **visited** Tokyo. *(She visited Tokyo first.)*

Yes / No question		Short answers	
Main clause	**Past time clause**	**Affirmative**	**Negative**
Did he **take** classes	**before** he **opened** the café?	Yes, he **did**.	No, he **didn't**.

Information question		Answer	
Main clause	**Past time clause**	**Subject**	**Verb**
What did he **do**	**after** he lost his job?	He	**started** a business.

Note: The time clause comes after a main clause or at the beginning of the sentence. The meaning does not change. When it is at the beginning of the sentence, put a comma at the end of the clause. ***Before** he opened the café, he took some classes.*

>> FOR PRACTICE, GO TO PAGE 126

3 PRONUNCIATION

A ▶01-10 Listen. Notice how we divide the sentences into thought groups. Then listen and repeat.

He took some **clȧsses** / before he opened the **cafė**.

He started his own **bu̇siness** / after he lost his **jȯb** / a few **mȯnths** ago.

> **Thought groups**
>
> We break long sentences into thought groups. Each thought group has a main stress. We often pause (stop) a little between each group.

B ▶01-11 Write a line (/) after each thought group. Then listen and check your answers.

1. I was really upset when I heard the news.
2. Did you learn Korean before you moved to Seoul?
3. I applied to graduate school after I quit my job.
4. She studied Italian for a year before she went to Italy.
5. We moved to a house in the country after we had the baby.

C PAIRS Practice saying the sentences in 3B. Underline the main stress in each thought group.

4 CONVERSATION

A ▶01-12 Listen or watch. Put a checkmark (✓) next to the correct name.

	Living with parents	Started a business	Lost his job	Quit his job	Took business classes
Eddie					
Mark					

B ▶01-13 Listen or watch. Complete the conversation.

Sarah: How's your brother?

Mario: OK. He quit his job _____ his office moved.

Sarah: Oh. That's too bad.

Mario: Yeah. He's doing all right. How's your husband?

Sarah: He's great. He started his own business _____ he took some classes.

Mario: Wow! Good for him.

C ▶01-14 Listen and repeat. Then practice with a partner.

D PAIRS Make new conversations. Use these words or your own ideas.

> lost his job
> changed careers

5 TRY IT YOURSELF

A MAKE IT PERSONAL Think about what your family's been doing. Complete the chart.

	when	
	after	
	before	

B PAIRS Talk about your family. Ask questions to get more information.

A: My sister got engaged after she graduated from college.

B: That's great. When is she getting married?

☐ I CAN TALK ABOUT MY FAMILY.

SARAH GOLD
@SarahG

The weekend is finally here.
Excited to see my favorite city!

1 VOCABULARY Tourist activities

A ▶01-15 Listen. Then listen and repeat.

TRAVEL
BOOK
CONTACT

go to a concert

go to a play

go to a restaurant

go to a museum

go sightseeing

go souvenir shopping

go on a tour

B Write one activity from 1A under each picture. Some pictures can have more than one activity.

1. _____ 2. _____ 3. _____ 4. _____ 5. _____

C PAIRS Imagine you're going on vacation to Vienna, Shanghai, or another major city. Look at the activities in 1A. Which activity would you want to do most? Why?

I'd want to go souvenir shopping because...

2 GRAMMAR Suggestions with *Let's* and *Why don't*

Let's	Not	Base form of verb	Why don't	Subject	Base form of verb
Let's		**go** sightseeing.	Why don't	you	**try** a bus tour?
	not	**spend** too much money.		we	**meet** by the elevator?

>> FOR PRACTICE, GO TO PAGE 127

3 CONVERSATION

A ▶01-17 Listen or watch. Circle the correct answers.

1. What is Sarah doing on Friday?
   a. She's meeting a friend.
   b. She's going home.
   c. She's going souvenir shopping.
2. When do Sarah and Mario plan to go on a tour?
   a. before souvenir shopping
   b. after dinner
   c. before the conference
3. Who does Sarah need to shop for?
   a. herself
   b. her friends
   c. her family
4. What's the problem with their dinner plans?
   a. They can't agree on a restaurant.
   b. The restaurant is booked.
   c. The restaurant is closed.

B ▶01-18 Listen or watch. Complete the conversation.

Mario:	Do you want to go sightseeing tonight?
Sarah:	Sorry, I have plans. _____ we do something tomorrow?
Mario:	Sure. What do you want to do?
Sarah:	_____ go on a tour.
Mario:	OK. That sounds great.

C ▶01-19 Listen and repeat. Then practice with a partner.

D PAIRS Make new conversations. Use the words in 1A or your own ideas.

4 TRY IT YOURSELF

A MAKE IT PERSONAL Think of something fun to do in your city. Complete the chart.

What to do	Details

B PAIRS Invite your partner. Make a suggestion about what to do. Ask questions to get more information.
A: Let's go to the free concert on Friday.
B: Sure. Where is the concert?
A: It's downtown. Why don't we take the bus together?
B: OK. That sounds great.

C CLASS Report to the class. What places or activities did you talk about?

☐ I CAN MAKE AND RESPOND TO INVITATIONS.

SARAH GOLD
@SarahG

How important is it to have friends at work? Check out this article. You might be surprised!

1 BEFORE YOU READ

A   PAIRS   Do you or did you have friends at work? Were they important to you? Talk about them.

I had a few friends at my last job. My friend Amy was...

B   VOCABULARY   ▶01-20 Listen. Then listen and repeat.

friendship   research   employees   workplace   encourage

>> FOR PRACTICE, GO TO PAGE 155

2 READ

A   Read the Reading Skill. Look at the title. Which answer best describes the topic?

a. how to find a job
b. making new friends
c. friendships at work

> **READING SKILL** Find the topic
>
> The *topic* is what an article is about. When you know the topic before you begin reading, it is easier to understand the article. One way to find the topic is to think about the title.

B   ▶01-21 Listen. Read the article.

DO FRIENDSHIPS WORK AT WORK?

Many people around the world spend a lot of time at work. In fact, they spend more time with co-workers than with friends and family. With all the time we spend at our jobs, does it make a difference to us or to our
5   employers if we become friends with our co-workers?

Research shows that employees are 50 percent happier with their jobs when they have friends at work. And for that reason, they're more likely to work harder and be loyal to their companies. A recent article in the
10   *Harvard Business Review* highlights the importance of friendships in the workplace. According to the article, "Friendships at Work," these friendships help to create "a common sense of purpose and the mentality that we are in it together."

15   Many companies are starting to see the value of friendships in the workplace and have thought of some interesting ways to help build these friendships. For example, Zappos, the online shoe company, has a very special way to make sure its employees think
20   about friendship. Every time employees log on to their computers, they see a picture of another employee. Then they are asked some questions. *How well do you know this person? Do you just say hello? Do you spend time together after work? Are you really good friends?* In

25   this way, Zappos asks employees to think about the other people in the office. "My hope," says Zappos owner Tony Hsieh, "is that we can have more employees who plan to be close friends." The company also
30   encourages everything from cookouts to bowling parties. They believe that people who know each other better will work together better.

Other companies also work hard to help
35   their employees make friends. Google is famous for encouraging friendships at work. The company has game rooms, a rock climbing wall, a gym, and a swimming pool. They even have restaurants with free food so that employees can spend time together. Employee Camille James
40   moved from Tokyo to California to work for Google. She belongs to a bowling team and a salsa dance group at the company. She says that they help "break down the walls" that can happen in a large organization.

Research shows that people stay longer at companies and
45   are better employees when they have friends at work. So, when you're looking for your next job, look for a company that encourages people to have friends at work. You will probably like your job more, and you'll be a better employee!

3 CHECK YOUR UNDERSTANDING

A Read the article again. What is the article mainly about?

   a. how all tech companies are helping employees to be better workers

   b. the importance of friendships at work and what some companies are doing

   c. which companies are the best to work for if you're looking to make new friends

B Read the article again. Circle the correct answers.

1. People are more loyal to their companies when they have ___ at work.

   a. friends   b. free food   c. more vacations

2. Research about friendships at work shows that people ___ .

   a. aren't interested in having friends at work

   b. feel more involved when they have friends at work

   c. don't work hard when they have too many friends at work

3. Zappos asks its employees if they know each other so that ___ .

   a. they think about who they know at work

   b. the company can learn more about their employees

   c. managers know about friendships at the company

4. Camille James joined the bowling team to ___ .

   a. get more exercise   b. get to know people   c. learn a new sport

5. Zappos and Google encourage friendships at work by ___ .

   a. giving away free food

   b. providing a gym where people can meet

   c. planning fun events for employees

C FOCUS ON LANGUAGE Reread lines 34-43 in the article. Think about the phrases *famous for* and *break down the walls*. Circle the correct answers.

1. The expression *famous for* means ___ .

   a. well-known for

   b. loved for

   c. not known for

2. The expression *break down the walls* means to ___ .

   a. change offices to make them more open

   b. help people get to know each other

   c. help people find new jobs at other companies

D PAIRS What was the article about? Retell the most important ideas. Use your own words.

4 MAKE IT PERSONAL

Find other companies that encourage friendships at work.

A Think about your friends. Where did you meet them? Was it at school, at a job, or somewhere else? How did you meet? Complete the chart.

Friend's name	Where did you meet?	How did you meet?

B PAIRS Compare your charts. Did you meet your friends at the same kinds of places?

☐ I CAN READ ABOUT WORK FRIENDSHIPS.

SARAH GOLD
@SarahG

My friend is visiting Toronto next month. Any ideas for things we could do?

1 BEFORE YOU WRITE

A Think about a time when a friend visited you for a few days. What did you see and do?

B Read Sarah's email. How does Sarah feel about Maria's visit?

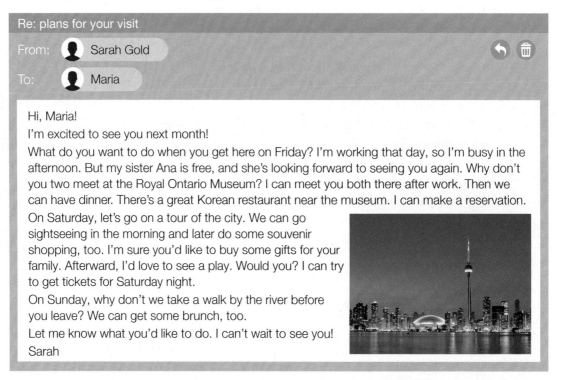

Re: plans for your visit

From: Sarah Gold

To: Maria

Hi, Maria!

I'm excited to see you next month!

What do you want to do when you get here on Friday? I'm working that day, so I'm busy in the afternoon. But my sister Ana is free, and she's looking forward to seeing you again. Why don't you two meet at the Royal Ontario Museum? I can meet you both there after work. Then we can have dinner. There's a great Korean restaurant near the museum. I can make a reservation.

On Saturday, let's go on a tour of the city. We can go sightseeing in the morning and later do some souvenir shopping, too. I'm sure you'd like to buy some gifts for your family. Afterward, I'd love to see a play. Would you? I can try to get tickets for Saturday night.

On Sunday, why don't we take a walk by the river before you leave? We can get some brunch, too.

Let me know what you'd like to do. I can't wait to see you!

Sarah

C Read the email again. What do you think of Sarah's suggestions? What things would you or wouldn't you like to do? Complete the chart.

Things I like	Things I don't like

2 FOCUS ON WRITING

A Read the Writing Skill.

> **WRITING SKILL** Use transition words for time
>
> Transition words for time can show *when* something happened. Use these words to make your writing clearer. Then the reader will know the order events happened.
>
> Transition words for time include: *while, after, when, during, next, then, so far, later, soon, sometimes, afterward, following, whenever,* etc.
>
> Look at this example: *I went to the store. Then I had some lunch. Later, I went to the library. While I was at the library, I saw José.*

B Reread Sarah's email. Underline all the transition words for time.

C Read the email again. Complete the chart. Write the activities from the email in the order they will happen.

Friday	Saturday	Sunday
Arrive in Ontario		

3 PLAN YOUR WRITING

A Your friend wants to visit you for the weekend. Where will you go? What will you do? Write the activities in order.

Friday	Saturday	Sunday

B PAIRS Tell your partner about your plans.

On Saturday morning, we will go to a nice restaurant and have breakfast. Then we will go for a walk in the park.

4 WRITE

Write an email to your friend using your plans from 3A. Remember to use transition words for time. Use the email in 1B as a model.

5 REVISE YOUR WRITING

A PAIRS Exchange emails and read your partner's email.
1. Underline all the transition words for time.
2. Did your partner explain the plans in order?
3. Did your partner include information for all three days?

B PAIRS Can your partner improve his or her email? Make suggestions.

6 PROOFREAD

Read your email again. Can you improve your writing?

Check your
• spelling
• punctuation
• capitalization

☐ I CAN WRITE AN EMAIL TO MAKE PLANS.

PUT IT TOGETHER

1 MEDIA PROJECT

A ▶01-22 Listen or watch. What is Yu talking about?

B ▶01-22 Listen or watch again. Answer the questions.

1. What is Yu doing these days? _____

   _____

2. Where is Yu living these days? _____

3. What does Yu do on the weekends? _____

C Show your own photos.

Step 1 Think about what you've been doing lately. Choose 3-4 photos that show what activities you are doing or no longer doing.

Step 2 Show your photos to the class. Talk about the activities.

Step 3 Answer questions about your photos. Get feedback on your presentation.

> Where are you living these days?

> I'm still living with my parents.

2 LEARNING STRATEGY

LEARN GRAMMAR IN PHRASES AND SENTENCES
Choose a grammar point that you want to learn. Practice the grammar point in phrases and sentences to help you speak more fluently. Write phrases and sentences using this grammar in your notebook. Read them aloud to memorize them.

Find grammar phrases in the unit that help listeners understand connections between ideas. For example, *these days* helps listeners know that you're talking about what you've been doing lately. Write a sentence with each phrase to practice. Read the sentences aloud when you study.

3 REFLECT AND PLAN

A Look back through the unit. Check (✓) the things you learned. Highlight the things you need to learn.

Speaking objectives
- [ ] Talk about what you're doing
- [ ] Talk about your family
- [ ] Make and respond to invitations

Vocabulary
- [ ] Activities
- [ ] Life events
- [ ] Tourist activities

Pronunciation
- [ ] Main stress
- [ ] Thought groups

Grammar
- [ ] Present continuous for temporary situations
- [ ] Simple past + *when*, *before*, and *after*
- [ ] Suggestions with *Let's* and *Why don't*

Reading
- [ ] Find the topic

Writing
- [ ] Use transition words for time

B What will you do to learn the things you highlighted? For example, use your app, review your Student Book, or do other practice. Make a plan.

> Notes   Done
>
> In the app, do the lesson 1 grammar practice: present continuous

2 WHAT DO YOU THINK?

LEARNING GOALS

In this unit, you
- ⊘ describe two similar things
- ⊘ describe personal traits
- ⊘ talk about how people do things
- ⊘ read about life-changing advice
- ⊘ write a recommendation

GET STARTED

A Read the unit title and learning goals.

B Look at the photo of a team meeting. What do you see?

C Now read Eric's message. What does Eric mean when he says that he's "excited, but a little nervous?"

ERIC PARK
@EricP

I'm in charge of my first big project.
I'm excited, but a little nervous.

17

ERIC PARK
@EricP

First meeting about my new project today. Hope it goes well!

1 VOCABULARY Sensory verbs

A ▶02-01 **Listen. Then listen and repeat.**

look

The view **looks** beautiful.

taste

The dessert **tastes** sweet.

feel

The sweater **feels** soft.

smell

The sneaker **smells** bad.

sound

The music **sounds** terrible.

B **Look at the pictures. Complete the sentences with sensory verbs from 1A.**

silk

butter

a coconut

a fire alarm

a movie star

1. My new silk shirt _____ soft.
2. Butter _____ delicious on fresh bread.
3. This coconut _____ fresh.

4. The fire alarm _____ very loud!
5. Wow! That movie star _____ beautiful.

2 GRAMMAR Sensory verbs + *like*

COACH

Use *like* after sensory verbs to show that two things are similar.

Subject	Sensory verb	*Like*	Object
The shampoo	**smells**		coconuts.
Your hair	**feels**		silk.
They	**look**	like	movie stars.
Her alarm	**sounds**		a bird.
This butter	**tastes**		garlic.

Notes

- Use *a little* or *a lot* before *like* to express the degree of similarity.
  *She looks **a little like** her mother. This tofu tastes **a lot like** chicken.*
- Sensory verbs express states, not actions. Do not use sensory verbs or other non-action verbs in the present continuous tense.
  *My room **smells** like flowers. **not** My room is smelling like flowers.*

>> FOR PRACTICE, GO TO PAGE 128

3 PRONUNCIATION

COACH

A ▶02-03 Listen. Notice the /s/ or /z/ sound of the underlined letter *s*. Then listen and repeat.

/s/ <u>s</u>oft look<u>s</u>   /z/ ea<u>s</u>y feel<u>s</u>

B ▶02-04 Listen. Notice the sound of the underlined *s*. Circle the word that does *not* have the sound shown. Then listen and repeat.

1. /s/   <u>s</u>ilk   <u>s</u>ure   <u>s</u>weet   <u>s</u>mell   3. /s/   like<u>s</u>   ta<u>s</u>te<u>s</u>   deliciou<u>s</u>   flower<u>s</u>
2. /z/   sound<u>s</u>   smell<u>s</u>   thi<u>s</u>   the<u>s</u>e   4. /z/   bu<u>s</u>y   mu<u>s</u>ic   u<u>s</u>ually   report<u>s</u>

C PAIRS Practice the words in 3B. Then practice the sentences in the grammar chart.

4 CONVERSATION

A ▶02-05 Listen or watch. Circle the correct answers.

1. Eric and Lucas are working on ___.
   a. a new shampoo   b. an advertisement   c. a drawing
2. Eric doesn't want honey in his hair because it doesn't ___.
   a. taste good   b. smell good   c. feel good
3. Lucas ___ a woman on the beach.
   a. draws   b. finds a picture of   c. writes about

B ▶02-06 Listen or watch. Complete the conversation.

Eric: How would you describe the shampoo?
Lucas: How about this? It _____ coconuts, and it feels like silk.
Eric: Hmm. I'm not so sure. What about, after you use it, your *hair* _____ silk.
Lucas: That's better. What else could we say?
Eric: How about, use it and you'll _____ a movie star?
Lucas: Good idea!

CONVERSATION SKILL Express disagreement

To express disagreement, say: *I disagree.*, *I don't agree.*, *I don't think so.*, *I hate to disagree (with you), but…*, *I'm not so sure (about that).*, *I don't know (about that).*, or *I wouldn't say that.*

A: This tastes like chicken.
B: I disagree.

Listen to or watch the conversation in 4A again. Underline the words that you hear above.

C ▶02-07 Listen and repeat. Then practice with a partner.

D PAIRS Make new conversations. Use these words or your own ideas.

candy   peaches   rock star   model

5 TRY IT YOURSELF

A GAME Student A, describe something. Don't say what it is. Student B, guess what your partner is describing.

A: It smells like coconuts, and it feels like…
B: Is it a…?

B WALK AROUND Continue the game. Describe things for your classmates. Report to the class. Who guessed what you were describing?

■ I CAN DESCRIBE TWO SIMILAR THINGS.

ERIC PARK
@EricP

The people on my project team are from five countries. That's a lot of time zones!

 1 VOCABULARY Attitudes

A ▶02-08 **Listen. Then listen and repeat.**

difficult

eager

delighted

proud

willing

determined

afraid

ashamed

B ▶02-09 **Listen to the descriptions of people's attitudes. Write one word from 1A to match each description.**

1. _____   3. _____   5. _____
2. _____   4. _____   6. _____

C PAIRS Student A, describe yourself or someone else using one of the words from 1A. Student B, guess the word.

A: I work hard and study a lot.
B: Determined.

2 GRAMMAR *Be* + adjective + infinitive

Infinitives can follow certain adjectives that describe reactions and feelings.

Subject	Be	Adjective	Infinitive
She	is	eager	to help.
They	are	easy	to work with.
It	is	hard	to reach them.

Notes
- Use adverbs of frequency before adjectives.
  He's always eager to help. It's sometimes hard to reach them.
- Use contractions, such as *she's, they're, it's,* etc., in spoken English and informal writing.

Be careful! Not all adjectives can be followed by an infinitive.

Common adjectives followed by infinitives: *happy, delighted, glad, sad, afraid, ashamed, eager, excited, surprised, shocked, proud, ready, difficult, hard, easy, lucky, willing*

>> FOR PRACTICE, GO TO PAGE 129

3 PRONUNCIATION

Ⓐ ▶02-11 **Listen. Notice the number of syllables and the stress. Then listen and repeat.**

• •	• •	• • •	• • •
eager	afraid	amazing	personal

Ⓑ ▶02-12 **Listen. Write each adjective in the correct column in 3A. Then listen and check your answers.**

ashamed	creative	willing	practical
nervous	negative	special	delicious

Ⓒ PAIRS **Make three sentences using the words in 3A and 3B.**

4 CONVERSATION

Ⓐ ▶02-13 **Listen or watch. Circle T for *True* and F for *False*. Correct the false statements.**

1. Eric and Min-ji are talking about a new product.   T   F
2. Eric enjoys working with Lucas because he is a talented illustrator.   T   F
3. Eric isn't happy with the new freelancers' work.   T   F
4. Eric can talk to the freelancers in Colombia anytime.   T   F
5. It's possible to work at many different locations at TSW Media.   T   F

Ⓑ ▶02-14 **Listen or watch. Complete the conversation.**

Min-ji: How's the project going?

Eric: It's going well! Lucas is a _____ guy. He's always eager to help.

Min-ji: Oh, good. And what are the new freelancers like?

Eric: They're very _____ , and they have a lot of creative ideas.

Min-ji: I'm happy to hear that. I know the old freelancers were difficult to work with.

Ⓒ ▶02-15 **Listen and repeat. Then practice with a partner.**

Ⓓ PAIRS **Make new conversations. Use these words or your own ideas.**

willing to share ideas
afraid to ask questions

5 TRY IT YOURSELF

Ⓐ MAKE IT PERSONAL **Think about one of your friends. What is he or she like? Take notes.**

Ⓑ PAIRS **Talk about your friend. Describe his or her personal traits. Ask questions.**

A: My friend Beto is great. He's always willing to help me.
B: Oh yeah? How so?

■ I CAN DESCRIBE PERSONAL TRAITS.

ERIC PARK
@EricP

75% of employees think feedback is important, but only 30% say they get it. I need to spend more time on this!

1 VOCABULARY Adverbs of manner

A ▶02-16 Listen. Then listen and repeat.

> **well:** behaving or doing something in a good way
> **quickly:** moving or doing something fast
> **easily:** moving or doing something comfortably
> **carefully:** moving or doing something without making mistakes
> **badly:** behaving or doing something in a way that is not good
> **slowly:** moving or doing something at a low speed
> **honestly:** behaving or doing something in an honest and fair way
> **carelessly:** behaving or doing something without thinking

B Put the adverbs from 1A into the correct categories.

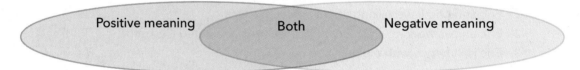

Positive meaning   Both   Negative meaning

C PAIRS Student A, say an adverb from 1A. Student B, say what can be done this way.

A: easily   **B:** ride a bike

2 GRAMMAR Adverbs of degree and manner

COACH

Adverbs modify verbs. Adverbs can also modify adjectives and other adverbs. Adverbs of degree show *intensity*. Adverbs of manner show *how* something happens.

Subject	Verb	Object	Adverb of degree	Adverb of manner
Yoko	speaks	English	**fairly**	**well**.
The manager	spoke		**very**	**honestly**.

Adverbs of degree
- Use *fairly* or *pretty* to weaken an adverb. *She speaks English **fairly** well. = Her English is OK.*
- Use *really, very,* or *extremely* to strengthen an adverb. *She speaks English **really** well. = Her English is excellent.*

Adverbs of manner: Most adverbs of manner are formed with an adjective + -ly. If the adjective ends with a *y*, change the *y* to *i*.

Adverbs formed with adjective + -ly	
bad	badly
careful	carefully
careless	carelessly
easy	easily
honest	honestly
quick	quickly

Same adjective and adverb form	
fast	fast
hard	hard
late	late

Irregular adverbs	
good	well

>> FOR PRACTICE, GO TO PAGE 130

3 LISTENING

A ▶02-18 Listen to the podcast. Circle the correct answer.

Managers give feedback to employees to ___ .
a. tell them they are working badly
b. help improve their performance
c. get to know them

B ▶02-18 Read the Listening Skill. Listen again. Listen for words that signal paraphrasing. Complete the sentences.

> **LISTENING SKILL** **Listen for paraphrasing**
>
> When you are listening to a speaker, pay attention to words that signal paraphrasing. Speakers use these words to explain something in a different way. Some of these signal words include *in other words, or, that is, which is,* and *which means.*

1. Employee feedback, _____ information about how well someone is working, is important.
2. Ask employees for feedback about their work. _____ , let them give feedback to you.
3. If you start with something positive, employees will be more open to what you have to say, _____ they will listen to your ideas.
4. Follow up with your employees. _____ , talk to them again.

C ▶02-18 Listen again. Look at the poster. Complete the sentences with the missing words.

EFFECTIVE FEEDBACK

Think about your _____ before giving feedback.

Let good _____ give you feedback.

Make a _____ with your employees.

Begin with something _____ .

Don't give a poor employee too much _____ feedback.

Tell your employee what he or she isn't doing well.

Have a _____ message.

Give specific suggestions.

Follow up with your employee in a few _____ .

D PAIRS What are the three best suggestions on the poster in 3C? Discuss.

4 TRY IT YOURSELF

A MAKE IT PERSONAL Look at the vocabulary in 1A. Write one sentence about yourself for four of the words.

B PAIRS Talk about yourself using your notes from 4A. Ask questions to get more information.
A: I love to go running. I run very quickly.
B: Oh, really? Where do you like to run?

C WALK AROUND Continue the conversation. Talk to three classmates. Report to the class. How did your classmates answer? Were any of your answers similar?

■ I CAN TALK ABOUT HOW PEOPLE DO THINGS.

ERIC PARK
@EricP

Best advice I ever got from my dad:
The harder you try, the luckier you get.

1 BEFORE YOU READ

A   PAIRS   Think about a time when you gave someone advice. What was it? Did this person take your advice? How did that make you feel?

I gave my sister some advice last week. I told her she should look for a new job and...

B   VOCABULARY   ▶02-19 Listen. Then listen and repeat.

> **a piece of advice**: a suggestion about what to do
> **a designer**: someone who draws or plans new things
> **a product**: something that people grow or make and then sell
> **recycled**: changed so that it can be used again
> **elegant**: simple and beautiful
> **wise**: able to make good choices and give good advice

>> **FOR PRACTICE, GO TO PAGE 155**

2 READ

A   PREVIEW   Look at the letter and the photograph. What do you think the letter is about?

B   ▶02-20 Listen. Read the letter to a newspaper editor.

To the editor:

I was very interested in your article about advice. I once got a piece of advice, and it changed my life.

I'm a designer. Ten years ago, I was designing my first product, and I was determined to show everyone how good I was. After a lot of
5   planning and hard work, I came up with a new design for a bag. The bag was made of recycled plastic bottles. It was black, and it looked and felt like leather. I thought my design was very elegant.

My first design job

Most of my co-workers really liked my design. However, one person, Lin, suggested a change. She thought the bag should come in bright colors that you can see in the dark.
10   "More and more people are running or bicycling after dark," she said, "and bright colors could be very popular with them. This could be a huge seller." I didn't even want to think about Lin's idea. I knew exactly what my bag should look like and exactly what would sell.

That evening I had dinner with my favorite teacher from design school. I told her all about my bag and mentioned Lin's suggestion. I thought my teacher was very wise, and I expected her to tell me how right
15   I was and how wrong Lin was. Instead, she smiled at me and said, "If you think you know something, find someone who disagrees and listen to them."

At first I was upset, but after I thought about it, I understood. I had been so excited by my own idea that I wasn't willing to listen to anyone else. But Lin's suggestion would make the bag useful to a bigger group of buyers. It also made the bag safer. I decided to include her idea in my presentation to the head of my
20   company. And guess what? He loved it! He even said his favorite part of the design was the bright colors!

Over the past ten years, I have often remembered my teacher's advice. Without it, my company might not have chosen to sell my bag. But more importantly, it taught me how important it is to just listen. So remember, be open to advice from other people, even if you don't agree with them at first. You never know how that advice might change your life!

25   Sincerely,
Elena Mays

3 CHECK YOUR UNDERSTANDING

A Read the Reading Skill. Answer the questions.

1. Read the letter. Underline the sentence that tells you the main idea.
2. Which statement best describes the main idea?
   a. People should be open to opinions and advice from others.
   b. Only listen to advice from people you trust and get along with.
   c. There are many different ways to give good advice.

> **READING SKILL** Find the main idea
>
> The main idea is the most important thought in a piece of writing. It is the topic plus what the writer wants to say about the topic. Sometimes the main idea is stated at the beginning of a text but it may also appear elsewhere in the text. When you read, ask yourself: "What is the text about?" and then, "What does the writer want to tell me about the topic?"

B Read the letter again. Circle the correct answers.

1. Elena wrote this letter to the editor to ___ .
   a. show people that she is smart
   b. sell more of her bags
   c. share some helpful advice
2. This bag was very important to Elena because ___ .
   a. she was excited that her co-workers liked the design
   b. she believed that this was her best idea as a designer
   c. she wanted to show that she was a good designer
3. Lin's suggestion made the bag ___ and easier to sell.
   a. more elegant   b. useful to more people   c. cheaper to make
4. Her teacher's advice helped Elena because ___ .
   a. it made her more open to other people's ideas
   b. it made her feel bad about her own design
   c. it made her feel better about her own ideas

C FOCUS ON LANGUAGE Reread lines 10-11 in the letter. Think about the phrases *after dark* and *huge seller*. Circle the correct answers.

1. The expression *after dark* means **without lights / at night / in black clothes**.
2. The phrase *huge seller* means **sold in big sizes / sold in large numbers / sold at high prices**.

D PAIRS What is the letter about? Retell the most important ideas in the letter. Use your own words.

The letter is about how a woman got some advice and...

> Find other articles about advice and how it has helped people. 🔍

4 MAKE IT PERSONAL

A Think about a time when you were given advice. What was the advice? Who gave it to you? Was it good or bad advice? How did it affect you? Complete the chart.

Advice	Person	Good / Bad	What happened

B PAIRS Tell your partner about the advice you were given. Explain how it did or didn't help you.

My parents gave me great advice about... They said...

▣ I CAN READ ABOUT LIFE-CHANGING ADVICE.

LESSON 5   WRITE A RECOMMENDATION

1 BEFORE YOU WRITE

A Think about a time when you needed a
recommendation. For example, when you
applied to a university or applied for a job.
What kinds of things were included in the recommendation?

B Read Eric's recommendation on an employment website. How does Eric feel about Lucas?

Eric Park
Copywriter

Lucas and I currently work together at TSW
Media. We work together a lot, and we are
involved in many of the same projects. I
am delighted to write this recommendation
for him.

Lucas is a talented illustrator. He is very
creative, and his graphics help to make our
ads successful. Lucas is especially good at
working with different technologies. His hand
drawings are beautiful, but he also creates
amazing artwork using computer programs,

such as Illustrator. He is smart, hard-working,
and very determined. He works quickly and
carefully, and he is always willing to help on
different projects when needed.

Lucas is extremely well-liked by his co-
workers and by all our clients. He works well
with others, and he is always eager to share
his ideas. Lucas is a great team member, and
he is a real asset to our team. We're lucky to
have him.

C Read the recommendation again. How does Eric organize his recommendation?
Complete the chart.

Paragraph 1 *How does he know this person?*	Eric knows Lucas from TSW Media.
Paragraph 2 *What skills does this person have?*	talented illustrator
Paragraph 3 *How does this person get along with others?*	well-liked

2 FOCUS ON WRITING

A Read the Writing Skill.

B Look at three incorrect sentences from Eric's first draft of his recommendation. Underline the correct versions in the model.

1. Lucas and I currently work together at TSW Media we work together a lot, and we are involved in many of the same projects.
2. A talented illustrator.
3. His hand drawings are beautiful, he also creates amazing artwork using computer programs, such as Illustrator.

> **WRITING SKILL** Write complete sentences in formal writing
>
> In formal writing, we need to write complete sentences.
> - Complete sentences need to have a subject and a verb.
> - Complete sentences need to be separated or connected in some way.
>   - Use a period, not a comma, to separate complete sentences.
>   - Use a conjunction, such as *and*, *but*, *or*, or *so*, to connect complete sentences.

C Look at the sentences in 2B again. What were the mistakes? How did he fix them?

3 PLAN YOUR WRITING

A You need to write a recommendation for a classmate or co-worker. Think of someone to write about. Complete the chart.

Paragraph 1 *How do you know this person?*	
Paragraph 2 *What skills does this person have?*	
Paragraph 3 *How does this person get along with others?*	

B PAIRS Talk to your partner about your ideas for your recommendation.

I am writing about... We met at...

4 WRITE

Write a recommendation using your ideas from 3A. Remember to use complete sentences. Use the recommendation in 1B as a model.

5 REVISE YOUR WRITING

A PAIRS Exchange recommendations and read your partner's.
1. Did your partner explain how they know the person?
2. Did your partner describe the person's skills and personality?
3. Did your partner use complete sentences?

B PAIRS Can your partner improve his or her recommendation? Make suggestions.

Check your
- spelling
- punctuation
- capitalization

6 PROOFREAD

Read your recommendation again. Can you improve your writing?

☐ I CAN WRITE A RECOMMENDATION.

PUT IT TOGETHER

1 MEDIA PROJECT

A ▶02-21 **Listen or watch. What kind of product does Fatma describe?**

B ▶02-21 **Listen or watch again. Answer the questions.**

1. What's the name of the product? _____

2. What three reasons does Fatma give? _____
   _____

3. What's one detail for each of the three reasons?
   _____
   _____

C Make your own video.

Step 1 Think of a product that you own and that you like.

Step 2 Make a 30-second video. Describe the product and say the reasons why you like it. Give details about the product.

Step 3 Share your video. Answer questions and get feedback.

2 LEARNING STRATEGY

> **DESCRIBE WHAT YOU SEE**
>
> Learn new vocabulary by describing people and things around you. What words do you know? Look up words you don't know. Write sentences to help you learn the new words.

It smells like coconuts.

Review the descriptive words in the vocabulary. Try to use these words to describe people and things around you. For example, use sensory verbs (*look, feel, smell, taste, sound*). Write five descriptive sentences for practice. Review the sentences twice a week.

3 REFLECT AND PLAN

A Look back through the unit. Check (✓) the things you learned. Highlight the things you need to learn.

Speaking objectives
- ☐ Describe two similar things
- ☐ Describe personal traits
- ☐ Talk about how people do things

Vocabulary
- ☐ Sensory verbs
- ☐ Attitudes
- ☐ Adverbs of manner

Pronunciation
- ☐ The letter *s*
- ☐ Syllables and stress

Grammar
- ☐ Sensory verbs + *like*
- ☐ *Be* + adjective + infinitive
- ☐ Adverbs of degree and manner

Reading
- ☐ Find the main idea

Writing
- ☐ Write complete sentences in formal writing

B What will you do to learn the things you highlighted? For example, use your app, review your Student Book, or do other practice. Make a plan.

< Notes   Done

In the app, do the Lesson 1 vocabulary practice: Sensory verbs
_____
_____
_____

3 HOW WAS YOUR WEEKEND?

LEARNING GOALS

In this unit, you
- ⊘ express how you feel
- ⊘ talk about past activities
- ⊘ describe your emotions
- ⊘ read about extreme sports
- ⊘ write a description of a trip

GET STARTED

A Read the unit title and learning goals.

B Look at the photo of a park. What do you see?

C Now read Alba's message. What do you think she means by "I hope I can fit everything in!"?

ALBA PARDO
@AlbaP

Making plans for my weekend away. I hope I can fit everything in!

ALBA PARDO
@AlbaP

I never know how much to share when people ask me about my weekend. Is there a rule?

 1 VOCABULARY Participial adjectives

 ▶03-01 Listen. Then listen and repeat.

exciting	excited	boring	bored	surprising	surprised
It's **exciting**.	They're **excited**.	It's **boring**.	She's **bored**.	It's **surprising**.	He's **surprised**.
tiring	tired	embarrassing	embarrassed	relaxing	relaxed
It's **tiring**.	They're **tired**.	It's **embarrassing**.	She's **embarrassed**.	It's **relaxing**.	He's **relaxed**.

B Put the adjectives from 1A in the correct category.

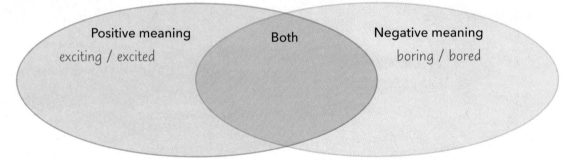

Positive meaning
exciting / excited

Both

Negative meaning
boring / bored

C PAIRS Compare your answers in 1B. Did you put the adjectives in the same categories?

 2 GRAMMAR Participial adjectives
COACH

The *-ing* and *-ed* forms of verbs can sometimes be used as adjectives.	
The weekend was really **exciting**.	We were really **excited**.
The city has **interesting** neighborhoods.	I'm **interested** in learning about them.

Notes
- Use the *-ing* form to show that someone or something caused a feeling.
- Use the *-ed* form to show how someone feels.

>> FOR PRACTICE, GO TO PAGE 131

3 PRONUNCIATION

A ▶03-03 Listen. Notice the pronunciation of *-ed*. Then listen and repeat.

/t/	/d/	/ɪd/
embarrass<u>ed</u>	bor<u>ed</u>	delight<u>ed</u>

The *-ed* ending in adjectives

The *-ed* ending in adjectives has three pronunciations. We pronounce *-ed* as an extra syllable /ɪd/ after the sound /t/ or /d/: *delighted*. After other sounds, the e in *-ed* is silent. We pronounce *-ed* as /t/ after voiceless sounds like /s/ and /k/: *embarrassed*. We pronounce *-ed* as /d/ after voiced sounds like /z/ and /r/: *bored*.

B ▶03-04 Listen. Write each adjective in the correct column in 3A. Then listen and check your answers.

1. I'm tired. 2. He felt ashamed. 3. We were relaxed. 4. They're excited.

C PAIRS Student A, say one of the adjectives in 3A or 3B. Student B, say something that makes you feel that way. **A:** relaxed **B:** I feel relaxed at the beach.

4 CONVERSATION

A ▶03-05 Listen or watch. Circle the correct answers.

1. Sarah thought the city had a lot of ___ neighborhoods.
   a. exciting   b. crowded   c. interesting
2. Sarah was embarrassed at the restaurant because ___ .
   a. she forgot her wallet
   b. she didn't know how to use chopsticks
   c. she wasn't hungry
3. On Sunday, Sarah ___ .
   a. went for a swim   b. went to a museum   c. went to dinner

B ▶03-06 Listen or watch. Complete the conversation.

Alba: How was your weekend?

Sarah: It was _____ . On Saturday, I went sightseeing and then I went souvenir shopping.

Alba: Oh, fun!

Sarah: And on Sunday, I had brunch with some friends. I'm _____ today.

Alba: I'll bet. Try to do something _____ tonight.

C ▶03-07 Listen and repeat. Then practice with a partner.

D PAIRS Make new conversations. Use the words from 1A to talk about how you felt.

I went hiking this weekend. It was really tiring.

5 TRY IT YOURSELF

A MAKE IT PERSONAL Think about the first time you did something. How did you feel?

B PAIRS Discuss your notes from 5A. Ask questions to get more information.

A: Last month, I took my first yoga class.
B: How did you like it?
A: I loved it. It was really relaxing.

■ I CAN EXPRESS HOW I FEEL.

LESSON 2   TALK ABOUT PAST ACTIVITIES

ALBA PARDO
@AlbaP

I really love this city! There's so much to see and do.

1 VOCABULARY Past participles

A ▶03-08 Listen. Then listen and repeat.

Regular verbs have the **same** form for the simple past and the past participle.

Base form of verb	Simple past	Past participle
work	worked	worked
study	studied	studied

Some irregular verbs also have the **same** form for the simple past and the past participle.

Base form of verb	Simple past	Past participle
have	had	had
make	made	made

Some irregular verbs have **different** forms for the simple past and past participle.

Base form of verb	Simple past	Past participle
be	was / were	been
do	did	done
go	went	gone
see	saw	seen

B PAIRS Student A, say the base form of a verb from 1A. Student B, say the past participle.

2 GRAMMAR Present perfect for past experiences

Use the present perfect to show that something has or hasn't happened at an indefinite time in the past. The present perfect is formed with *have* or *has* + past participle.

Questions			Statements			
Have / Has	Subject	Past participle	Subject	*Have / Has*	*Not*	Past participle
Have	you	**been** to the theater?	I	have		**been** to the theater.
Has	she	**seen** the play?	She	has		**seen** the play.
Have	they	**taken** a bus tour?	They	have	not	**taken** a bus tour.

Notes
- The adverbs *yet* and *already* are often used with the present perfect. Use *yet* in questions and negative statements. Use *already* in affirmative statements.
  *Have you seen the play **yet**? I haven't seen the play **yet**.*
  *She has **already** seen the play.* or *She has seen the play **already**.*
- It is possible to have more than one verb after *have* or *has*. It is not necessary to repeat *have* or *has*.
  *I **have traveled** to Paris and **have seen** the Eiffel Tower.*
  More common: *I **have traveled** to Paris and **seen** the Eiffel Tower.*
- Use the simple past when the specific time of the event is mentioned. *I **took** a tour **last week**.*

Use contractions, such as *haven't* or *hasn't*, in spoken English and informal writing.

>> FOR PRACTICE, GO TO PAGE 132

COACH 3 PRONUNCIATION

A ▶03-10 Listen. Notice the stressed words. Then listen and repeat.

What did you do on the weekend? I went for a walk in the park.

Have you been to the Botanical Gardens? No, I haven't.

Have you gone to the theater in New York? Yes, I have. It's amazing!

B ▶03-11 Listen. Underline the stressed words. Then listen and repeat.

1. A: Have you been to the zoo in Beijing?
   B: No, but I've heard it's great.

2. A: Have you gone to a concert in London?
   B: Yes, I have. I loved it!

C PAIRS Practice the conversations in 3A and 3B.

4 CONVERSATION

A ▶03-12 Listen or watch. Complete the sentences.

1. Alba had a _____ weekend.
2. On the weekend, Alba saw a _____ .
3. Alba _____ goes to the theater when she is in New York.
4. Sarah compares her trip to New York to a _____ .

B ▶03-13 Listen or watch. Complete the conversation.

Sarah: What did you do this weekend?

Alba: I went for a walk in the park. It was nice to do something outdoors.

Sarah: Oh, that reminds me. Have you been to the Botanical Gardens?

Alba: No, I haven't. I was planning to go, but _____ this week.

Sarah: Well, maybe next time. So, what else did you do?

Alba: I went to the theater. _____ ?

Sarah: No, I haven't but I'd like to go.

CONVERSATION SKILL
Change the topic

To change the topic in a conversation, say: *That reminds me…, Oh, did you hear…?, Incidentally…, Oh, before I forget…,* or *I don't mean to change the subject, but…*

A: Before I forget—I heard that you got a new job. Congratulations!

B: Thanks. I'm really busy, but I love it.

Listen to or watch the conversation in 4A again. Underline the words that you hear above.

C ▶03-14 Listen and repeat. Then practice with a partner.

D PAIRS Make new conversations. Use these words or your own ideas.

zoo
aquarium

5 TRY IT YOURSELF

A MAKE IT PERSONAL Think about things you've done or places you've been to in your country. Take notes.

B PAIRS Talk about the things or places from 5A. Ask questions to get more information.

A: Have you done anything interesting lately?
B: Yes, I have. I've been to the museum.

■ I CAN TALK ABOUT PAST ACTIVITIES.

ALBA PARDO
@AlbaP

Listen to this podcast. What a mystery! Some things just can't be explained…

 1 VOCABULARY Adjectives to describe feelings

A ▶03-15 Listen. Then listen and repeat.

| calm | happy | angry | upset |
| curious | lonely | disappointed | nervous |

B ▶03-16 Listen to the scenarios. Write a word from 1A to explain how they feel. More than one answer may be possible.

1. _____ 3. _____
2. _____ 4. _____

C PAIRS Student A, make up your own scenarios like the ones in 1B. Student B, say how you feel.

A: You just spent the day on the beach with your family. How do you feel?
B: I feel happy.

 2 GRAMMAR Ability / Inability in the past
COACH

Could and *be able to* are often used to express ability in the past. *Couldn't* and *not able to* are often used to express inability in the past.

Subject	*Could*	*Not*	Base form of verb	Subject	*Was / Were*	*Not*	*Able to*	Base form of verb
I			**read** the map.	I				**read** the map.
He	**could**		**sleep** that night.	He	was		**able to**	**sleep** that night.
We		**not**	**find** the trail.	We	were	**not**		**find** the trail.

Notes
- Use *be able to*, **not** *could,* to talk about one specific event in the past.
  *They **were finally able to find** a restaurant.*
  *I **was able to finish** my project last night.*
- It is possible to use the negative form *couldn't* for one specific event in the past. *Couldn't* and *wasn't / weren't able to* have the same meaning.
  *I **couldn't find** the restaurant.*   *I **wasn't able to find** the restaurant.*
- Use contractions, such as *couldn't* or *wasn't / weren't*, in spoken English and informal writing.

>> FOR PRACTICE, GO TO PAGE 133

3 LISTENING

Ⓐ ▶03-18 Listen to the podcast. Circle the correct answer.

Tony and Jack were both scared when they ___ .
a. got lost   b. arrived in town   c. saw the photo

Ⓑ ▶03-18 Read the Listening Skill. Listen again. Complete the phrases with the descriptions you hear.

1. The town looked like a really _____ .
2. Tony is a very _____ guy.
3. The restaurant was decorated with lots of old _____ .
4. Tony sat _____ looking around the room.

Ⓒ ▶03-18 Listen again. Circle the correct answers.

1. Jin and Tony felt ___ when they saw the town.
   a. curious   b. bored   c. disappointed
2. Tony was ___ when they got to the town.
   a. angry   b. upset   c. happy
3. The restaurant was ___ .
   a. dark   b. bright   c. loud
4. The man in the photo had the same ___ as Tony.
   a. clothes   b. scar   c. eye color
5. Tony wanted to ___ .
   a. order food   b. go home   c. return to the restaurant
6. Jin wasn't able to sleep that night because he was so ___ .
   a. excited   b. upset   c. frightened

Ⓓ PAIRS What do you think about the man in the photo? Who do you think he was?

> **LISTENING SKILL**
> **Listen for descriptions**
>
> A good story includes descriptions, so it's important to know how to listen for them. Descriptions tell you how something *looks, sounds, feels, tastes,* or *smells.*

4 TRY IT YOURSELF

Ⓐ MAKE IT PERSONAL Think about something frightening, surprising, or funny that happened to you. (You can also make up a story.) Think about what you could and couldn't do, and how that made you feel. Take notes.

Ⓑ PAIRS Tell your partner what happened. Ask questions to get more information.

A: Last year, I saw an old friend and I couldn't remember her name! I felt so embarrassed.
B: So, what happened?

Ⓒ WALK AROUND Share your story with three classmates. Complete the chart. Then report to the class. Whose story was the funniest, most surprising, or most frightening?

Name	What happened? What could / couldn't you do?	How did you feel?

☐ I CAN DESCRIBE MY EMOTIONS.

ALBA PARDO

@AlbaP

Want to know what kind of person jumps out of airplanes? You need to read this article.

1 BEFORE YOU READ

A PAIRS Extreme sports are activities that are very dangerous and exciting, like skydiving.
Do you or does anyone you know do extreme sports?

My friend likes cave diving. She...

B VOCABULARY ▶03-19 Listen. Then listen and repeat.

> **a risk-taker:** a person who does something that involves danger or chance
> **flight:** the act of flying through the air
> **an adrenaline rush:** a feeling that you have when you are excited, afraid, or in danger
> **in control:** able to make decisions and decide what should happen
> **out of control:** not able to make something happen the way you want
> **a fear:** the feeling of being afraid or very worried
> **focus:** to think about one thing only

>> **FOR PRACTICE, GO TO PAGE 155**

2 READ

A Read the Reading Skill. Scan the text for the unspoken words. Underline them.

B PREVIEW Look at the title and the photograph. What do you think the interview is about?

C ▶03-20 Listen. Read the interview.

> **READING SKILL** Notice text structure: Interviews
>
> Words that are not actually spoken during an interview are usually styled differently, such as in italics.

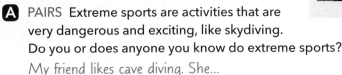

Extreme Sports and the Brain

BASE jumping: an extreme sport

Why do some people jump out of airplanes? Or ski off cliffs? Are they bored? Or do they just love danger?

I recently interviewed Marta Hu–a
5 *BASE jumper who also happens to be a psychologist who studies the brain–to learn more about these risk-takers.*

Dave Chin: Hi Marta, it's great to talk with you.
(DC)   Can you tell us what BASE jumping is?

10 **Marta Hu:** BASE jumping is a sport where people jump off of high places with only a special
(MH)   suit to help them fly. BASE stands for building, antenna, span (or bridge), and Earth.
     Each of these words represents a high object from which BASE jumpers start their flight.

DC: What can you tell us about people who do extreme sports, such as BASE jumping?

15 **MH:** Well, Dave, some people who do extreme sports can find everyday life boring and need
     to do something unusual to feel an adrenaline rush. When people do extreme sports, their
     brains create something called dopamine, which makes them feel happy.

DC: So, they need to do something that extreme just to feel some excitement?

MH: Well, they know that what they do is dangerous, so they don't take risks. BASE jumpers, for
20 example, learn everything they can about their equipment and the area where they will be
jumping. They are actually very smart, careful people who like to be in control.

DC: How could jumping off a cliff give someone control? I would feel totally out of control!

MH: Well, they need to be in control of their equipment, but mainly they are controlling their
fear. People have to focus and think very carefully about what they are doing. They describe
25 feeling very relaxed and peaceful.

DC: How does BASE jumping make you feel?

MH: When I jump, I see the world in a way that I can't on the ground. I push past my fear and I
focus. The jump only lasts 35 or 40 seconds, but time slows down, so it feels much longer.
In that moment, I feel 100% free.

3 CHECK YOUR UNDERSTANDING

A Which answer best describes the main idea of the interview?

People do extreme sports because ___ .

a. they are not afraid of anything

b. they find them relaxing

c. they feel intensely happy as a result

B Read the interview again. Circle the correct answers.

1. BASE jumping is ___ .
   a. jumping out of an airplane
   b. jumping without any equipment
   c. jumping from high objects

2. BASE jumpers are different than Dave expected because they ___ .
   a. are careful and plan their jumps
   b. love danger and like feeling afraid
   c. are bored with their lives

3. When BASE jumpers feel fear, they ___ .
   a. decide not to jump because it is too dangerous
   b. choose an even more dangerous jump
   c. focus and think about what they are doing

C FOCUS ON LANGUAGE Reread lines 27-29 in the interview. Think about the phrases *push past my fear* and *100%*. Circle the correct answers.

1. When Marta *pushes past her fear*, she ___ .
   a. moves to a better place to jump from
   b. feels afraid but jumps anyway
   c. thinks about the last jump she made

2. The expression *100%* means ___ .
   a. a little
   b. totally
   c. always

D PAIRS What is the interview about? Retell the most important ideas in the interview. Use your own words.

Find out about other extreme sports. 🔍

4 MAKE IT PERSONAL

A PAIRS Do you want to try an extreme sport, such as rock climbing, skydiving, or BASE jumping? Share your reasons with your partner.

I'd like to try rock climbing because...

B WALK AROUND Continue the conversation with your classmates. Report to the class. How do your classmates feel about extreme sports?

◼ I CAN READ ABOUT EXTREME SPORTS.

ALBA PARDO
@AlbaP

While I was away, I took a day trip to the small town of Cold Spring. Check out my post!

1 BEFORE YOU WRITE

A Think about a recent day trip.
Where did you go? What did you see and do?

B Read Alba's blog post. How did she feel about her trip?

Blog | About | Destinations | Contact

🔍 Search

A day trip

I just got back from a fun trip to NY. I had a great time and saw a lot of amazing things. I also went on a day trip while I was there. My co-worker, Laura, invited me to visit her hometown, Cold Spring, a small town on the river, north of the city. I haven't been to many places in the U.S., and it sounded nice. So, I decided to go there for the day.

We traveled to Cold Spring by train. The trip took a little over an hour, but the ride was nice and relaxing. The train went along the Hudson River, and the views were lovely. I was excited to explore somewhere new. We walked along the sparkling river and around the town. It was so charming! There were interesting shops and a large farmer's market with fresh fruits and vegetables.

We bought lunch at a local bakery and ate our sandwiches by the river. We watched the small boats go by, and I felt so calm. Then we went shopping, and I bought a beautiful book about flowers. We weren't able to do everything we wanted before we had to leave. But we had a great day, and I was happy to visit a new place.

Comment 💬

About
RSS Feed
Social Media
Recent Posts
Archives
Email

C Read the post again. Complete the chart.

Who went on the trip? Alba and her co-worker	Where did they go?
How did they get there?	Why did they go?
What did they do there?	Other details

2 FOCUS ON WRITING

A Read the Writing Skill.

B Reread Alba's post. Underline all the descriptive adjectives.

3 PLAN YOUR WRITING

A Think about a recent day trip you took. (Or you can make up your own story.) Complete the chart to plan your writing. Remember to include descriptive adjectives.

Who went on the trip?	Where did you go?
How did you get there?	Why did you go?
What did you do there?	Other details

B PAIRS Describe your trip to your partner.

Last month, I went on a day trip to...

4 WRITE

Write a post about a recent day trip you took using details from 3A. Remember to use descriptive adjectives. Use the post in 1B as a model.

5 REVISE YOUR WRITING

A PAIRS Exchange posts and read your partner's post.
1. Did your partner include details about his or her trip (*who, where, how, why, what*)?
2. Underline all the descriptive adjectives.
3. Did your partner's descriptive adjectives help you picture the trip he or she took? Why or why not?

B PAIRS Can your partner improve his or her post? Make suggestions.

6 PROOFREAD

Read your post again. Can you improve your writing?

Check your
• spelling
• punctuation
• capitalization

☐ I CAN WRITE A DESCRIPTION OF A TRIP.

PUT IT TOGETHER

1 MEDIA PROJECT

▶ **A** ▶03-21 Listen or watch. What does Ana talk about?

▶ **B** ▶03-21 Listen or watch again. Answer the questions.

1. How does Ana describe her weekend? _____

2. What two activities did Ana do? _____
   _____

3. What details does Ana give? _____
   _____
   _____

C Show your own photos.

Step 1 Think about a recent weekend. Choose 3-5 photos of what you did on the weekend.

Step 2 Show your photos to the class. Talk about your weekend. Describe what you did or saw.

Step 3 Answer questions about your photos. Get feedback on your presentation.

2 LEARNING STRATEGY

> **FLASHCARDS FOR PRONUNCIATION**
>
> Make flashcards with a pronunciation rule and example words to help you remember how to say them. When you study, try to say as many words as you can that follow the rule.

> Pronounce -ed as an extra syllable /ɪd/ after /t/ or /d/.

> adjectives
>
> excited
>
> ended

Make flashcards to help you remember the rules for pronouncing the -ed endings for adjectives. Use the symbols /t/, /d/, or /ɪd/ to help you remember the correct pronunciation. Say the example words out loud.

3 REFLECT AND PLAN

A Look back through the unit. Check (✓) the things you learned. Highlight the things you need to learn.

Speaking objectives
- ☐ Express how you feel
- ☐ Talk about past activities
- ☐ Describe your emotions

Vocabulary
- ☐ Participial adjectives
- ☐ Past participles
- ☐ Adjectives to describe feelings

Pronunciation
- ☐ The -ed ending in adjectives
- ☐ Stressed words

Grammar
- ☐ Participial adjectives
- ☐ Present perfect for past experiences
- ☐ Ability / Inability in the past

Reading
- ☐ Notice text structure: Interviews

Writing
- ☐ Use descriptive adjectives

B What will you do to learn the things you highlighted? For example, use your app, review your Student Book, or do other practice. Make a plan.

Notes   Done

In the app, watch the Pronunciation Coach video: The -ed ending in adjectives

_____
_____
_____
_____

4

WOULD YOU LIKE SOMETHING TO EAT?

LEARNING GOALS

In this unit, you
- ⊘ talk about food choices
- ⊘ talk about food customs
- ⊘ talk about what you have and need
- ⊘ read about the science of dessert
- ⊘ write about a holiday meal

GET STARTED

A Read the unit title and learning goals.

B Look at the photo of a meal. What do you see?

C Now read Mandy's message. What does she mean?

MANDY WILSON
@MandyW

I'm always hungry! Thank goodness it's so easy to find great food in my city.

MANDY WILSON
@MandyW

Just got out of a meeting. So hungry!
My stomach is making noises.

1 VOCABULARY Lunch foods

A ▶04-01 Listen. Then listen and repeat.

a garden salad | salad dressing | a grilled vegetable wrap | tomato soup | spinach and mushroom pasta

a veggie burger | ketchup | an oatmeal cookie | fruit salad | soda | iced tea | lemon

B Put the lunch foods from 1A in the correct category.

Starters	Mains	Desserts	Drinks	Condiments / Flavorings

C PAIRS Add one food to each category in 1B.

2 GRAMMAR Count and non-count nouns with *some*, *any*, and *no*

Count nouns		Non-count nouns	
Singular count nouns	**Plural count nouns**	tomato soup	ketchup
a tomato	two tomato**es**	fruit salad	salad dressing
an apple	some apple**s**		

Questions				Short answers	Answers with *some*, *any*, and *no*				
Are	there	**any**	burgers?	Yes. Yes, there are.	Yes,	there	are	**some**	burgers.
					No,	there	aren't	**any**	
					There	are	**no**		
Is			ketchup?	No. No, there isn't.	Yes,	there	is	**some**	ketchup.
					No,	there	isn't	**any**	
					There	is	**no**		

Notes
- Use *any* in questions and negative statements. Do not use *any* in affirmative statements.
- Do not use *no* with a negative verb.
- Many nouns have both a count and a non-count meaning.
  *I love **chocolate**.* (chocolate in general) *Do you want **a chocolate**?* (one piece of chocolate)

>> FOR PRACTICE, GO TO PAGE 134

3 PRONUNCIATION

COACH

A ▶04-03 Listen. Notice the dropped syllable. Then listen and repeat.

veg~~e~~table   choc~~o~~late   ev~~e~~rything

Dropped syllables

Some words have a vowel letter in the middle that is not usually pronounced. When we don't pronounce the vowel, the word loses, or drops, a syllable.

B ▶04-04 Listen. Draw a line (/) through the vowel letter that is *not* pronounced. Then listen and repeat.

1. favorite   2. different   3. evening   4. interested   5. family   6. comfortable

C PAIRS Student A, say a word from 3A or 3B. Student B, say the number of syllables.

4 CONVERSATION

A ▶04-05 Listen or watch. Circle the correct answers.

1. What does Mandy eat for lunch?
   a. salad and a roast beef sandwich
   b. tomato soup and salad
   c. a veggie burger and salad

2. Why doesn't Mario eat what Mandy offers him?
   a. He doesn't like soup.
   b. He doesn't like sandwiches.
   c. He doesn't like vegetables.

3. Why does Mario say, "I guess I do like vegetables."?
   a. because he tries some salad
   b. because he wants to be nice
   c. because the burger is made with vegetables

CONVERSATION SKILL Hesitate

Sometimes you need to hesitate in a conversation because you need time to think or you aren't sure about something. When you need to hesitate, say: *Well…, Um…, Hmm…, Let me think…, Let's see…,* or *You know…*

A: Are there any chicken sandwiches?
B: Let's see…No, there aren't any left.

Listen to or watch the conversation in 4A again. Underline the words that you hear above.

B ▶04-06 Listen or watch. Complete the conversation.

Mario: Let's have something to eat.

Mandy: OK. I'm going to have _____ salad. Would you like _____ ?

Mario: No, thanks. Are there _____ chicken sandwiches?

Mandy: Let's see. No, I'm sorry! There aren't _____ .

Mario: That's OK. Um…I think I'll have a burger.

C ▶04-07 Listen and repeat. Then practice with a partner.

D PAIRS Make new conversations. Use these words or your own ideas.

tomato soup
grilled vegetable wraps
cheese sandwich

5 TRY IT YOURSELF

A MAKE IT PERSONAL Plan a menu. Choose one food for each category in 1B. Take notes.

B PAIRS Talk about what you're going to eat.
A: Let's see…I'm going to have some fruit salad for dessert. What about you?
B: I'm going to have an oatmeal cookie.

■ I CAN TALK ABOUT FOOD CHOICES.

MANDY WILSON
@MandyW

There are places where almost everyone lives to 100. Can you guess what people eat there? Hint: It's not burgers!

 1 VOCABULARY Partitives

A ▶04-08 Listen. Then listen and repeat.

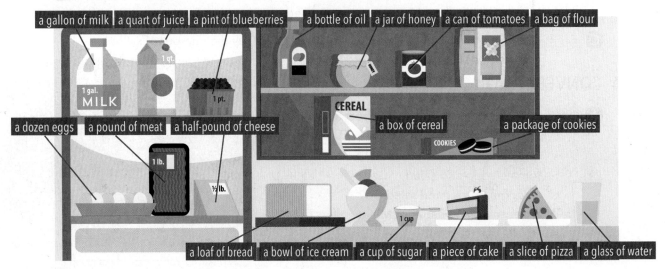

a gallon of milk | a quart of juice | a pint of blueberries | a bottle of oil | a jar of honey | a can of tomatoes | a bag of flour

a dozen eggs | a pound of meat | a half-pound of cheese | a box of cereal | a package of cookies

a loaf of bread | a bowl of ice cream | a cup of sugar | a piece of cake | a slice of pizza | a glass of water

B ▶04-09 Listen to the conversations. Write the words that you hear.

1. a _____ of tomatoes and a _____ of sugar
2. a _____ of ice cream and a _____ of cookies
3. a _____ of soda with a _____ of lemon
4. a _____ of blueberries and one _____ of butter

C PAIRS List a new food for five of the partitives in 1A.

a bottle of soda, a pound of butter,...

 2 GRAMMAR *Much / Many / A lot of* and *How much / How many*

COACH

Use *much* with non-count nouns. Use *many* with plural count nouns. Use *a lot of* with both non-count nouns and plural count nouns.

Questions with *How much / How many*				Statements with *Much / Many / A lot of*	
How much / How many	Noun			*Much / Many / A lot of*	Noun
How much	water	do you drink?	I drink	a lot of	water.
	meat	did she eat?	She didn't eat	much	meat.
How many	vegetables	did they cook?	They didn't cook	many	vegetables.

Notes
- We usually use *much* in questions and negative statements. Do not use *much* in affirmative statements. *I usually drink **a lot of water**.* not *I usually drink ~~much water~~*.
- *Many* and *a lot of* are often used the same way.
  *I like **many** different **vegetables**. I like **a lot of** different **vegetables**.*
- Use *how many* with words like *cartons, bottles, bags, pounds, bowls,* and *cups*.
  ***How much water** do you drink?* ***How many bottles of water** do you drink?*

>> FOR PRACTICE, GO TO PAGE 135

3 PRONUNCIATION

COACH

A ▶04-11 Listen. Notice the way we link *of* to the words around it. Then listen and repeat.

a piece of cake   a bowl of ice cream
a box of cookies   a box of oatmeal

> **Phrases with *of***
>
> The word *of* is unstressed and has the short, weak vowel /ə/. When the next word begins with a vowel sound, we say /əv/: *a cup of ice*. When the next word begins with a consonant sound, the /v/ sound is often dropped: *a glass of milk*. We link *of* to the words around it.

B ▶04-12 Draw a line (/) through *f* in *of* if we can drop the sound. Draw linking lines to show where we link *of* to the words around it. Then listen and check your answers.

1. a cup of coffee
2. a carton of eggs
3. a bowl of soup
4. a bottle of water
5. a glass of iced tea
6. a lot of oil

C PAIRS Make three sentences using the phrases in 3A or 3B. Link *of* to the words around it.

4 LISTENING

A ▶04-13 Listen to the podcast. What is it about?

a. the foods people grow in Sardinia and Okinawa
b. famous dishes from Sardinia and Okinawa
c. how food affects health in Sardinia and Okinawa

Centenarians in Okinawa and Sardinia

LISTENING SKILL Listen for comparisons

Speakers sometimes talk about two different things or situations. Listen for words that show comparisons, such as *both*, *also*, *similar*, *whereas*, and *alike*.

B ▶04-13 Read the Listening Skill. Listen again. Put a check mark (✓) under the things that people eat and drink in Sardinia and Okinawa, according to the speaker.

	Sweet potatoes	Vegetables	Soup	Tea	Wine	Water
Sardinia						
Okinawa						

C ▶04-13 Listen again. Complete the sentences.

1. A centenarian is _____ years old or older.
2. A person's _____ can help them live a long life.
3. Antioxidants help to _____ aging.
4. The biggest meal in Blue Zones is _____ of the day.

D PAIRS Which idea from the podcast do you think is the most important? Why?

5 TRY IT YOURSELF

A MAKE IT PERSONAL Think about your local foods and customs. What are the best healthy foods and drinks in your country? How much should you eat or drink every day? Take notes.

mangos; 1 cup per day

B PAIRS Discuss your notes from 5A. Ask questions to get more information.

A: Mangos are a big part of our local diet. It's important to eat a lot of fruits and vegetables.
B: I agree. How many mangos do you think you should eat?
A: I think you should eat one cup of mango every day.

☐ I CAN TALK ABOUT FOOD CUSTOMS.

MANDY WILSON
@MandyW

Some friends are coming over this weekend. What's the best barbecue food?

 1 VOCABULARY Food at a barbecue

A ▶04-14 Listen. Then listen and repeat.

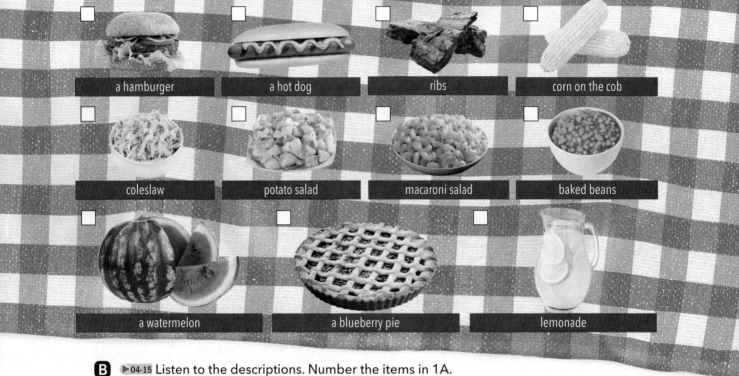

| a hamburger | a hot dog | ribs | corn on the cob |

| coleslaw | potato salad | macaroni salad | baked beans |

| a watermelon | a blueberry pie | lemonade |

B ▶04-15 Listen to the descriptions. Number the items in 1A.

C PAIRS Student A, choose a food from 1A or think of another barbecue food and describe it. Student B, guess the food.

A: It's a side dish. It's made with potatoes, mayonnaise, and cooked eggs.
B: Is it potato salad?

 2 GRAMMAR *Enough* and *Too much / Too many* + nouns
COACH

Enough + noun

	Not	*Enough*	Noun	
We have		**enough**	hamburgers.	We don't need any more.
There are	**not**	**enough**	hot dogs.	We need some more.

Note: *Enough* means the right amount. *Not enough* means less than you need.

Too much / Too many + noun

	Too Much / Too Many	Noun	
We have	**too much**	food.	We can't finish everything.
There are	**too many**	hamburgers.	We can't finish all of them.

Note: *Too much* and *too many* have negative meanings. They describe a quantity that is more than you need. Use *too much* with non-count nouns and *too many* with count nouns.

>> FOR PRACTICE, GO TO PAGE 136

3 CONVERSATION

A ▶04-17 Listen or watch. Circle the correct answers.

1. There are ___ hot dogs and ribs.
   a. enough   b. not enough   c. too many
2. Hailey and Mandy decide to buy ___ cans of beans.
   a. two   b. three   c. four
3. Mandy is a little mad at her sister because she ___ .
   a. invited too many people b. bought too much food c. forgot about the food
4. There will be ___ people at the barbecue.
   a. two   b. six   c. ten
5. They think Layla and Tom should bring ___ .
   a. potato salad and corn b. corn and coleslaw c. potato salad and blueberry pie

B ▶04-18 Listen or watch. Complete the conversation.

Hailey:	What do we need for the barbecue? I'm making a list.
Mandy:	We have _____ hamburgers. What about hot dogs?
Hailey:	OK. Hot dogs. What else?
Mandy:	Well, we need some corn on the cob. Let's get twelve.
Hailey:	That's too _____ . Let's get six. Anything else?
Mandy:	Coleslaw, potato salad, and macaroni salad.
Hailey:	That's too _____ food.

C ▶04-19 Listen and repeat. Then practice with a partner.

D PAIRS Make new conversations. Use the words in 1A or your own ideas.

4 TRY IT YOURSELF

A ROLE PLAY Plan a barbecue for six people. Write down four things you'll bring to the barbecue. Complete the chart.

Main	Side	Drink	Dessert

B PAIRS Compare your charts. Talk about what you have.
A: We have enough hot dogs and hamburgers.
B: Yes. And I think we have enough potato salad.

C PAIRS Talk about what you still need for the barbecue. Make a shopping list.
A: We need some watermelon. Let's get three.
B: That's too many watermelons. Let's get one.

☐ I CAN TALK ABOUT WHAT I HAVE AND NEED.

MANDY WILSON
@MandyW

I've often wondered why I ALWAYS find room for dessert. Now I know! 😊

1 BEFORE YOU READ

A PAIRS Do you like dessert? Have you ever eaten dessert even when you weren't hungry? Talk about it.

I love dessert! I...

B VOCABULARY ▶04-20 Listen. Then listen and repeat.

> **a bite:** a small piece of food that can easily fit in the mouth
> **room:** enough space
> **a sweet treat:** a dessert
> **taste:** the flavors you experience when you eat or drink something
> **pleasure:** the feeling of being happy or enjoying something
> **get used to:** to become comfortable with something, so that it does not seem new
> **satisfied:** pleased or happy
> **expand:** to become larger
> **push:** to move something away from you by pressing against it
> **relax:** to become looser; to become less tight

>> **FOR PRACTICE, GO TO PAGE 156**

2 READ

A PREVIEW Look at the title and the photograph. What do you think the article is about?

B ▶04-21 Listen. Read the article.

MAKE ROOM FOR DESSERT!

There's always room for a sweet treat!

Calories in Desserts

dessert	calories
1 slice of apple pie	411
1 slice of cheesecake	257
1 slice of chocolate cake	235
1 bowl of ice cream	267
1 slice of pecan pie	503

A calorie is a unit for measuring the amount of energy food will produce.

Picture this. You just finished eating a huge meal. You're so full your stomach hurts. You don't want to see another bite of food ever again! But then the dessert comes out, and it looks wonderful. Suddenly you think you can eat some more. Sound familiar? Well, you're not alone—we've all felt this way.
5 But have you ever wondered *why*? New research explains why we always have room for a sweet treat.

Dessert isn't boring—at least that's what our brains are telling us! When we eat something and like the taste, we feel pleasure. As we eat more, our brains get used to the flavor of that food, and we begin to feel less satisfied. Our
10 brains get bored of the food. It actually begins to lose its taste, and our brains tell us we're full. But if we eat food with a different flavor, such as dessert at the end of a meal, that new flavor "wakes our brains up" and we feel hungry again. Even if we're full, our brains tell us that we want that new flavor.

But our brains aren't the only reason we always have room for dessert. Our
15 stomachs actually *do* make more room. It's true! When we eat, our stomachs expand to make room for the food. When the food pushes against the walls of the stomach, we start to feel full. But sugar relaxes the walls of the stomach, so it can expand even more. And since most desserts have a lot of sugar, even if we're really full, the sugar in the dessert helps our stomachs make
20 more room.

We all might enjoy eating dessert, but remember, if we eat too much we can feel sick later. Scientists say we can solve this problem by having a small bite of dessert, rather than the whole thing. This way we satisfy our desire for a new flavor, but we don't eat too much. So, what do you have room for today?

3 CHECK YOUR UNDERSTANDING

A Which statement best describes the main idea of the article?

   a. Our brains and our bodies both make room for dessert.
   b. Everyone loves a sweet treat at the end of a meal.
   c. Eating the same kinds of food all the time is boring.

B Read the article again. Complete the sentences.

   1. When our brains get used to a food, we feel less _____ .
   2. Dessert appeals to our brains because the _____ .
   3. When we eat dessert, our stomachs expand because food _____ against the stomach and sugar _____ the walls of the stomach.
   4. Scientists say we should have a _____ instead of eating the whole dessert.

C FOCUS ON LANGUAGE Reread lines 1-2 in the article. Think about the words *picture this* and *full*. Then circle the correct answers.

   1. The expression *picture this* means ___ .
       a. to take a picture of something
       b. to imagine something
       c. to show someone a picture
   2. In this sentence, *full* means ___ .
       a. having a lot of something
       b. being happy
       c. having eaten enough

D Read the Reading Skill. Read the article again. Circle the main idea in each paragraph. Then underline one supporting detail in each paragraph.

> **READING SKILL** Identify supporting details
>
> Supporting details are facts and ideas that add more information to support the main idea. Supporting details can include examples, research, or quotes. Identifying these details can help you understand what the writer is trying to tell you.

E PAIRS What is the article about? Retell the most important ideas in the article. Use your own words.

   The article is about dessert and...

Find out about the science of other food groups. 🔍

4 MAKE IT PERSONAL

A Think about the article. Are there specific kinds of desserts or other types of foods that you always have room for? What are they? What makes the foods taste so good?

Type of food	Details

B PAIRS Tell your partner about the foods from 4A. Explain why the foods taste so good.

   I really like to eat...

☐ I CAN READ ABOUT THE SCIENCE OF DESSERT.

MANDY WILSON
@MandyW

My friend Alba wrote to me about a spicy sauce that's made with chili and chocolate. I've got to try that!

1 BEFORE YOU WRITE

A Think about a dish that is popular in your country. Why do you think it is popular? What are the ingredients?

B Read Alba's email. What does her family eat on Mexican Independence Day?

Re: Mexican Independence Day

From: Alba Pardo

To: Mandy

Hi, Mandy.

It's Independence Day in Mexico! Let me tell you about it. We usually celebrate with our family and friends. There's lots of music, dancing, and fireworks. And there's the food. We cook so much delicious food!

My family usually serves *molé chicken*, which is chicken in a spicy sauce made with chili and chocolate. We also have grilled corn with cheese and lime juice, and we have mangos with chili powder on top.

The most special dish is *chiles en nogada*. It's made with green peppers, meat, and spices. We top the peppers with a white sauce made from nuts, and we put some pomegranate seeds on top. This dish is always served on Independence Day because it has all the colors of the Mexican flag. The peppers are green, the sauce is white, and the pomegranate seeds are red.

For dessert, we have *tres leches* cake, which is made with three different kinds of milk. Tres leches means "three milks" in English. It's my favorite part of the meal!

How does your country celebrate Independence Day? I'd love to hear about it!

Alba

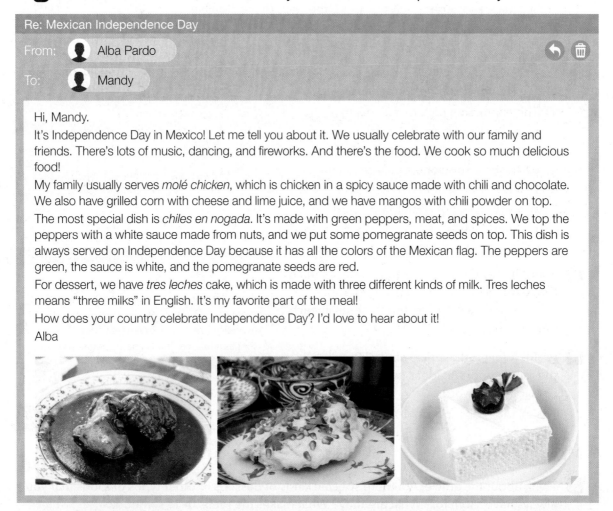

C Read the email again. Complete the chart with details from the email.

Food	Ingredients
molé chicken	chicken in a spicy sauce made with chili and chocolate
grilled corn	
mangos	
chiles en nogada	
tres leches cake	

2 FOCUS ON WRITING

(A) Read the Writing Skill.

(B) Look at these two sentences from the email in 1B. Look at the sentence openings and structures. Notice the differences.

And there's the food.

My family usually serves *molé chicken*, which is chicken in a spicy sauce made with chili and chocolate.

(C) PAIRS Find one more simple sentence, compound sentence, and complex sentence in the email in 1B. Underline the sentences in the email.

> **WRITING SKILL Add sentence variety**
>
> Use different sentence styles and structures in your writing. Doing this makes your writing more interesting and reduces repetition. There are several sentence patterns in English:
>
> - **Simple sentences:** a subject + verb + object (also called an independent clause). *My family usually serves* molé chicken.
> - **Compound sentences:** two independent clauses connected by a coordinating conjunction, like *and, but, so,* and *or. We top the peppers with a white sauce made from nuts, and we put some pomegranate seeds on top.*
> - **Complex sentences:** an independent clause + a dependent clause; a dependent clause can refer to the subject (*who, which*), the sequence / time (*since, while*), or the causal elements (*because, if*) of the independent clause. *This dish is always served on Independence Day because it has all the colors of the Mexican flag.*

3 PLAN YOUR WRITING

(A) Think about your favorite holiday. What foods are served on this holiday? List the foods and any interesting ingredients or details in the chart to help plan your writing.

Food	Ingredients / Details

(B) PAIRS Describe the foods that are served on your favorite holiday.

My favorite holiday is... We always eat...

4 WRITE

Write an email about the foods that are served on your favorite holiday. Use your ideas from 3A to help you. Remember to use a variety of sentences when you write. Use the email in 1B as a model.

5 REVISE YOUR WRITING

(A) PAIRS Exchange emails and read your partner's.

1. Did your partner include details about his or her favorite foods?
2. Did your partner use a variety of sentence types?
3. Did this make the email more interesting to read?

(B) PAIRS Can your partner improve his or her email? Make suggestions.

Check your
- spelling
- punctuation
- capitalization

6 PROOFREAD

Read your email again. Can you improve your writing?

■ I CAN **WRITE ABOUT A HOLIDAY MEAL.**

PUT IT TOGETHER

1 MEDIA PROJECT

 A ▶04-22 Listen or watch. What does Yu-jin talk about?

 B ▶04-22 Listen or watch again. Answer the questions.

1. What does Yu-jin want to cook? _____

2. What does she have? _____
   _____
   _____

3. What does she need? _____

C Make your own video.

Step 1 Choose a dish you want to cook. Think about what you need to make it.

Step 2 Make a 30-second video. Show the food you have in your cupboard or refrigerator.
Talk about what you have and what ingredients you still need.

Step 3 Share your video. Answer questions and get feedback.

2 LEARNING STRATEGY

USE GRAMMAR ON FLASHCARDS

Sometimes vocabulary is related to grammar. For example, you need to memorize the past tense of irregular verbs (*did*, *was*, *were*, etc.). When you make flashcards for vocabulary, also include grammar. Write an example sentence to help you study. Make new flashcards for 3–5 items a week.

> <u>Bread</u>
>
> non-count: Is there any bread?

Review the count and non-count nouns in the unit. What words do you need to learn?
Make five flashcards with the words and the unit's grammar. Include example sentences for each flashcard. Review the cards twice a week.

3 REFLECT AND PLAN

A Look back through the unit. Check (✓) the things you learned. Highlight the things you need to learn.

Speaking objectives
- [ ] Talk about food choices
- [ ] Talk about food customs
- [ ] Talk about what you have and need

Vocabulary
- [ ] Lunch foods
- [ ] Partitives
- [ ] Food at a barbecue

Pronunciation
- [ ] Dropped syllables
- [ ] Phrases with *of*

Grammar
- [ ] Count and non-count nouns with *some*, *any*, and *no*
- [ ] *Much / Many / A lot of* and *How much / How many*
- [ ] *Enough* and *Too much / Too many* + nouns

Reading
- [ ] Identify supporting details

Writing
- [ ] Use sentence variety

B What will you do to learn the things you highlighted? For example, use your app, review your Student Book, or do other practice. Make a plan.

Notes | Done
Review the grammar chart in lesson 1, page 42.

5 WHEN CAN WE MEET?

LEARNING GOALS

In this unit, you
- ⊙ make and respond to suggestions
- ⊙ identify problems and solutions
- ⊙ talk about what you need to do
- ⊙ read about 3D printing
- ⊙ write advice on how to manage your time

GET STARTED

A Read the unit title and learning goals.

B Look at the photo of a conference call. What do you see?

C Now read Lucas's message. How does Lucas have meetings with people in so many places?

LUCAS MORALES
@LucasM

I love that I can have meetings with people all over the world—and never leave Costa Rica!

LUCAS MORALES
@LucasM

I love technology when it works, but when it doesn't… 😕

 1 VOCABULARY Technology at work

A ▶05-01 **Listen. Then listen and repeat.**

| unplug a cable | add a wireless network | check the [Wi Fi] connection | click a link |

| download a program | connect to a projector | restart the computer | call tech(nical) support |

B Look at the situations below. Circle the next step for each situation.

1. You want to use the Internet.
   a. Add a wireless network.
   b. Download a program.
2. You need to show a presentation.
   a. Check the connection.
   b. Connect to a projector.

3. Your computer screen suddenly won't change.
   a. Unplug a cable.
   b. Restart the computer.
4. You're at work and your computer won't start.
   a. Call tech support.
   b. Click a link.

C PAIRS Brainstorm. Look at the actions in 1A. List two-three reasons why you do them.

unplug a cable: to disconnect from a printer,…

 2 GRAMMAR *Could* and *should* for suggestions

COACH

Use *could* and *should* to make suggestions. *Should* is stronger than *could*.

Questions				Statements			
Wh-word	**Should**	**Subject**	**Base form of verb**	**Subject**	**Should / Could**	**Not**	**Base form of verb**
Who	should	I	call?	You	could		**call** tech support.
What	should	she	do?	She	should		**restart** her computer.
						not	**unplug** the cable.

Notes
- Use *should* for questions and negative statements. Do not use the negative form *couldn't* for statements when making a suggestion.
- Use contractions, such as *shouldn't*, in spoken English and informal writing.

>> FOR PRACTICE, GO TO PAGE 137

3 PRONUNCIATION

COACH

A ▶05-03 Listen. Notice the consonant group at the beginning or end of these words. Then listen and repeat.

fi<u>x</u> the <u>pr</u>oblem   conne<u>ct</u> to the <u>scr</u>een   <u>cl</u>ose the <u>pr</u>ogram
<u>cl</u>ick the li<u>nk</u>   <u>pl</u>ug in the <u>sp</u>eakers   <u>st</u>art the <u>pr</u>esentation

> **Consonant groups**
>
> Many English words start or end with groups of two or three consonant sounds. We say the consonants in a group closely together.

B ▶05-04 Write a word from 3A that has the consonant group shown. The symbols on the left show sounds, not spellings. Then listen and check your answers.

1. /kl/ <u>click</u>, _____
2. /st/ _____
3. /pr/ _____
4. /skr/ _____
5. /ks/ _____
6. /kt/ _____
7. /ŋk/ _____
8. /pl/ _____
9. /sp/ _____

C PAIRS Practice the phrases in 3A. Are any of the consonant groups difficult for you? Can you think of other words that start or end with these consonant groups?

4 CONVERSATION

A ▶05-05 Listen or watch. Circle the correct answers.

1. After closing the presentation, Eric **restarts / shuts down / unplugs** the computer.
2. Eric **plugs in the cable / clicks a link / adds a wireless network** before he tries to connect.
3. Eric **connects to the screen / checks the sound / starts the presentation** last.
4. To join the meeting, people need to **open a file / download a program / call tech support**.

B ▶05-06 Listen or watch. Complete the conversation.

Eric:	I can't get our presentation to play. What _____ I do?
Lucas:	You _____ unplug the cable. Then plug it in again.
Eric:	Uh-huh.
Lucas:	If that doesn't fix the problem, you _____ restart your computer.
Eric:	Got it.

> **CONVERSATION SKILL** Show you understand
>
> To show that you understand what someone is saying in a conversation, say: *OK, Uh-huh, I understand,* or *(I've) got it.*
>
> **A:** Now, shut down your computer.
> **B:** Got it.
>
> Listen to or watch the conversation in 4A again. Underline the words that you hear above.

C ▶05-07 Listen and repeat. Then practice with a partner.

D PAIRS Make new conversations. Use these words or your own ideas.

download the new program   call tech support

5 TRY IT YOURSELF

A MAKE IT PERSONAL Think of something that you want to do with technology. Take notes.

B PAIRS Student A, say what you want to do with technology. Student B, suggest an idea or solution. Then change roles.

A: I want to edit my vacation photos. What should I use?
B: You could download this photo app.

☐ I CAN MAKE AND RESPOND TO SUGGESTIONS.

LESSON 2 IDENTIFY PROBLEMS AND SOLUTIONS

LUCAS MORALES
@LucasM

Tech support to the rescue!

 1 VOCABULARY Technology issues and hardware

A ▶05-08 Listen. Then listen and repeat.

The screen is frozen.

The sound isn't working.

a screen | a monitor | a microphone | headphones | a speaker

I can't make a video call.

My computer keeps crashing.

I can't get online.

a webcam | a hard drive | a keyboard | a mouse

B ▶05-09 Listen to the problems. Number the technology issues in 1A.

C PAIRS Look at the hardware in 1A. Which of these items can freeze, stop working, or crash? What other items can also have these issues?

A: A monitor can stop working.   **B:** A cell phone can stop working, too.

 2 GRAMMAR *Will, may,* and *might* to express likelihood

Use *will* to talk about something that is certain to be true in the future. Use *may* or *might* when you are unsure of something.

Subject	Will / May / Might	Not	Base form of verb
It	will		**solve** the problem.
		not	
You	may		**be** connected to the Internet.
		not	
The problem	might		**happen** again.
		not	

Notes
- Use *will (most / very) likely* or *will probably* to talk about something that is expected to be true.
  That **will most likely** solve the problem.
  That **won't likely** solve the problem. That **likely won't** solve the problem.
  That **will probably** solve the problem. That **probably won't** solve the problem.
- Use *will definitely* to talk about something that is going to happen for sure.
  We **will definitely** be there tomorrow. We **definitely won't** be there tomorrow.

>> FOR PRACTICE, GO TO PAGE 138

3 LISTENING

A ▶05-11 Listen to the phone messages. Who leaves a message in all the conversations?

  a. someone from Tech Support

  b. someone from Reception

  c. employees with problems

B ▶05-11 Read the Listening Skill. Listen again. Circle the correct answers.

1. How can Yuki fix her speakers?
   a. unplug the cable and restart the computer
   b. click on the sound icon and change the volume level
   c. unplug and then plug in the speaker cables
2. What problem is Tom having?
   a. His laptop won't start.
   b. He can't log in.
   c. His screen stopped working.
3. What does Sarah have to do after she adds a wireless network?
   a. restart the computer
   b. check the password
   c. connect to the Internet

> **LISTENING SKILL** Listen for instructions
>
> Speakers often use certain phrases to explain instructions. Some of these phrases are *First,…, To start,…, Then,…, After that,…, Next…,* and *And finally…*

4. What should Sam do if Carla isn't free?
   a. call Junior in Tech Support
   b. call someone else in Reception
   c. cancel her presentation
5. What does Julio need to do as a last step?
   a. restart the computer
   b. delete some programs
   c. delete some files
6. What does Katie need to do first?
   a. turn on the speaker
   b. check the webcam
   c. plug in the cables correctly

C PAIRS Do you know another way to solve the problems in 3B? Tell your partner what you know.

4 TRY IT YOURSELF

A MAKE IT PERSONAL Think of a problem using one of the hardware items from 1A. Take notes.

B ROLE PLAY Student A, say the problem. Student B say what you think the cause is and suggest a solution.

A: My webcam doesn't work.
B: It may be because it's turned off. To start, check to see that it's on.

C WALK AROUND Continue the Role Play with your classmates. Take notes in the chart. Report to the class. Choose one response. Say the problem, the cause, and the solution.

Name	Problem	Solution

■ I CAN IDENTIFY PROBLEMS AND SOLUTIONS.

LUCAS MORALES
@LucasM

Lots of meetings with the design team this week, presenting ideas to clients. Wish me luck!

1 VOCABULARY Meeting preparation

A ▶05-12 **Listen. Then listen and repeat.**

send an invitation

write an agenda

reserve a meeting room

create a presentation

arrange a video call

order refreshments

make photocopies

check equipment

B You are planning a meeting. Put the actions from 1A in the order that you need to complete them. More than one answer may be possible.

2. _____   4. _____   6. _____   8. _____

1. _____   3. _____   5. _____   7. _____

C PAIRS Compare your answers in 1B. Did you put the actions in the same order?

2 GRAMMAR *Have to / Need to* for obligation and necessity

COACH

Affirmative statements			Negative statements				
Subject	*Have to / Need to*	Base form of verb	Subject	*Do / Does*	*Not*	*Have to / Need to*	Base form of verb
I	have to	make photocopies.	I	do		have to	make photocopies.
He	has to		He	does			
She	needs to	order lunch.	She	does	not	need to	order lunch.
They	need to		They	do			

Yes / No question				Short answers	
Do	Subject	*Have to / Need to*	Base form of verb	Affirmative	Negative
Do	I	have to	be there early?	Yes, you **do**.	No, you **don't**.

Information question					Answer		
Wh- word	*Do*	Subject	*Have to / Need to*	Base form of verb	Subject	*Have to / Need to*	Base form of verb
What	do	we	need to	bring?	You	need to	bring your laptops.

>> FOR PRACTICE, GO TO PAGE 139

3 PRONUNCIATION

A ▶05-14 Listen. Notice the weak pronunciation of *to* and the blended pronunciation of *have to*. Then listen and repeat.

> **Weak and blended pronunciation of *to***
>
> The word *to* is usually unstressed and has the short, weak pronunciation /tə/, especially before a consonant sound. Sometimes we blend *to* with the word before it. We blend *have to* together as "hafta" /hæftə/.

Are they coming to the office? I have to check the sound.

I need to call tech support.   I don't have to go to the meeting.

B ▶05-15 The word *to* is missing from these sentences. Write the word *to* where you think it is missing. Then listen and check your answers.

1. What do we need do?
2. I have write an agenda.
3. I need send invitations the guests.

4. I'll have send a link the website.
5. I don't have time do everything.
6. I don't need make photocopies.

C PAIRS List three things you have to or need to do this week. Share your list.

4 CONVERSATION

A ▶05-16 Listen or watch. Circle the correct answers.

1. New clients are **coming to the office** / *having a video conference* / *visiting a resort*.
2. Marta will help Victor **send an invitation** / *write an agenda* / *check the equipment*.
3. Lucas needs to **create a presentation** / *send an invitation* / *make a list of people*.
4. Lucas needs to order **lunch** / *breakfast* / *snacks*.
5. The meeting is **moved earlier** / *moved to next week* / *canceled*.

B ▶05-17 Listen or watch. Complete the conversation.

Victor: Let's talk about what we need to do for the meeting.

Lucas: Sure. I guess I _____ reserve a meeting room.

Victor: Yes, that's right.

Lucas: OK. Do I have to create a presentation?

Victor: No, you _____ . I'm going to do it.

Lucas: Is there anything else?

Victor: Yes. We _____ order refreshments.

C ▶05-18 Listen and repeat. Then practice with a partner.

D PAIRS Make new conversations. Use the words in 1A or your own ideas.

5 TRY IT YOURSELF

A MAKE IT PERSONAL You're going to plan a meeting. Think about what you'll need to do. Take notes.

B PAIRS Plan a meeting. Talk about what you need to do, and then decide on two things each of you will do.

A: We need to reserve a meeting room.
B: OK. I'll reserve the room. Do we have to...?

■ I CAN TALK ABOUT WHAT I NEED TO DO.

LUCAS MORALES
@LucasM

3D printing is going to change the world!

1 BEFORE YOU READ

A PAIRS What do you know about 3D printing?

3D printing is when...

B VOCABULARY ▶05-19 Listen. Then listen and repeat.

three-dimensional	a disaster	natural resources	waste

organs

skin	the lungs	the heart	a cell

>> FOR PRACTICE, GO TO PAGE 156

2 READ

A PREVIEW Look at the title and the photograph. What do you think the article is about?

B ▶05-20 Listen. Read the article.

3D PRINTING: A WHOLE NEW WORLD

Most people today know about 3D printers. These are machines that "print" three-dimensional objects from a computer program. The objects are built using thousands of tiny little slices. The slices are layered together to form a solid object. At first,
5 3D printers only made small, simple plastic objects. But the technology behind them is improving every day. So, what will we be "printing" in the future?

New Ways to Make Food
Today, many people do not have enough food, but 3D printing
10 will soon be able to help. Scientists are creating new 3D-printed foods which could be given to people without food, such as those who have been through a disaster. 3D foods can be made with the vitamins and minerals that people need to be healthy using ingredients that are grown quickly and easily. For example,
15 different types of plants like algae and grass. These foods can also be designed so that they are easy to move and deliver.

New Ways to Build
There are places around the world where it is hard to find a clean and inexpensive place to live. In addition, a lot of natural
20 resources are used in traditional building. But scientists have found a way to build homes with the help of a huge 3D printer. These homes are cheaper but still strong, and produce less

waste. In China, an entire 3D-printed house was
25 made in one month. In the future, all new homes might be made with 3D printers.

New Ways to Save Lives
30 The strangest and most exciting area of 3D printing could be medicine. Today, we are able to print medical equipment,
35 prosthetics, like artificial arms and legs, and even skin! But we could do so much more. Take organs, for example. They're not always available, so people often have to wait a long time for one. But someday, doctors might be able to print out a new lung for someone or even a new heart if the "ink" of a 3D printer
40 was made of cells.

Clearly the future of 3D printing is so much more than simple plastic objects. Someday, 3D printing will likely be involved in every part of our lives!

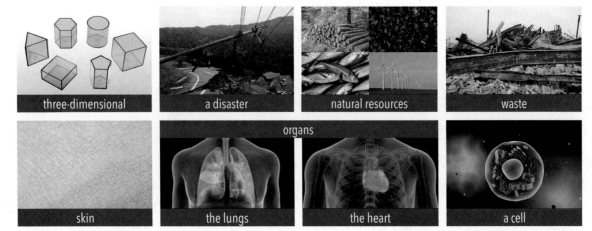

3D printers can make many different kinds of objects.

3 CHECK YOUR UNDERSTANDING

A Which statement best describes the main idea of the article?
   a. 3D printing is a fun way to create small plastic objects.
   b. 3D printing can change the way we do many things.
   c. 3D printing is a technology that has been completely developed.

B Read the article again. Complete the sentences.
   1. 3D-printed food can be made out of _____ like algae and grass.
   2. 3D-printed houses are less _____ and produce less _____ .
   3. When 3D printers use _____ as the ink, they will be able to print _____ like a new lung or heart.
   4. 3D printing will change _____ because it will help heal people.

C FOCUS ON LANGUAGE Reread lines 5-7 in the article. Think about the words *behind* and *"printing"*. Then answer the questions.
   1. What does the word *behind* mean in this sentence? _____
   _____
   2. Why is the word *"printing"* in quotation marks? What does it mean in this sentence?
   _____

D Read the Reading Skill. Read the article again. Identify the problems and solutions the author describes. How could the solutions help?

> **READING SKILL** Identify text structure: Problem / Solution
>
> Texts are organized in different ways depending on what they are describing and want to explain. One way to organize a text is to introduce a problem and then describe the solution to that problem.

Problems	Solutions	How the solutions could help

E PAIRS What is the article about? Retell the most important ideas in the article. Use your own words. The article is about 3D printing and how...

4 MAKE IT PERSONAL

Find out about what else 3D printers can do. 🔍

A Think about the article. Are there other kinds of problems you think 3D printing could solve? How do you think the solutions could help?

Problems	Solutions	How the solutions could help

B PAIRS Tell your partner about the problems and solutions. Discuss how you think 3D printing could solve these problems. I think 3D printing could solve the problem of...

■ I CAN READ ABOUT 3D PRINTING.

LESSON 5   WRITE ADVICE ON HOW TO MANAGE YOUR TIME

LUCAS MORALES
@LucasM

How much time do you spend on your device each day? How much is too much?

1 BEFORE YOU WRITE

A Do you ever feel like it's hard to stop checking your phone? What kind of advice would you give someone who spends too much time on his or her device?

B Cara posted a question on social media. Her friend Lucas responded with some advice. Read the post. Why does Lucas think he can help Cara?

  ←   Home | Profile | Logout

Cara Thompson
I spend way too much time on my phone. Any tips for how to avoid this?

Lucas Morales
Hi, Cara. I think I can help with your problem. Last year, I spent almost all my time on my devices, too. I was always online, reading my friends' posts. But then a friend told me a few things that I could do to help me spend less time online. Her advice really helped.

First, never take your phone to bed. Charge your phone in the kitchen or living room instead. Then you won't be tempted to go online. Next, always shut down your computer when you finish working. You'll be less likely to log in to your favorite sites even for just a minute. And last, try to leave your phone in another room sometimes. Frequently, when I'm spending time with my family or friends, I just don't take my phone with me.

I think these ideas will help. There are probably a lot more online, but remember, don't spend too much time looking for them. ;)

C Read the post again. What advice does Lucas give Cara? Take notes in the chart.

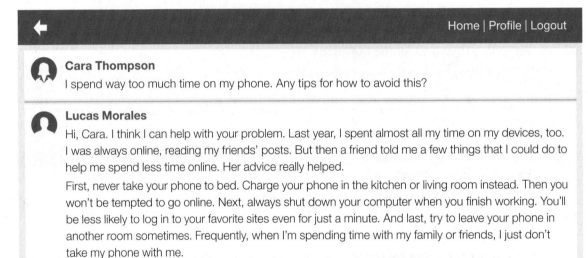

	Advice / Details
Problem	Advice / Details
	Advice / Details

2 FOCUS ON WRITING

A Read the Writing Skill.

B Reread the post. Underline the qualifiers.

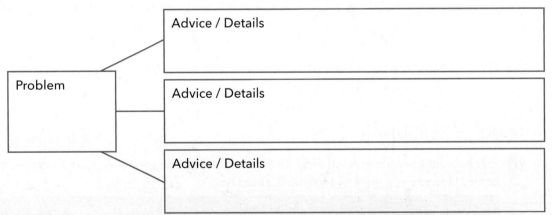

> **WRITING SKILL Use qualifiers**
>
> Qualifiers are words or phrases that limit or add to another word's meaning. Qualifiers can make a word stronger (*I spoke <u>very</u> quickly*) or weaker (*He's <u>a little</u> tired*). They give information about things like time (*He's <u>always</u> late*) or quantity (*I like <u>most</u> of my teachers*). Common qualifiers are: *very, quite, more, rather, pretty, really, so, nearly, almost, fairly, somewhat, least, less, a bit, kind of, a little, always, frequently, rarely, seldom, never, sometimes, every, most, few, all, a lot, many.*

3 PLAN YOUR WRITING

A Choose one problem below. Think about the problem. What could this person do to spend less time on his or her device? What advice could you give him or her?

> 1. Lee can't stop playing games on his tablet. His family is upset with him.
> 2. Ann is constantly using her phone to post on social media. She's failing her classes.
> 3. Rita watches videos online all day at work. She never finishes her work on time.

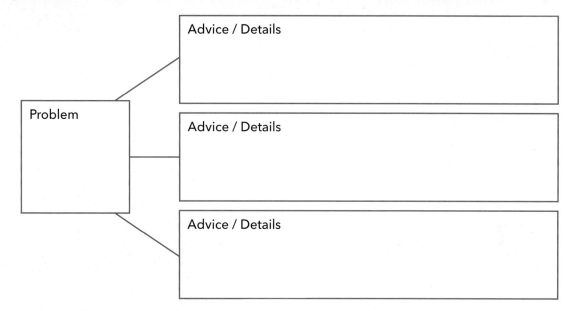

Problem	Advice / Details
	Advice / Details
	Advice / Details

B PAIRS Describe your advice to your partner.

I think Lee should...

4 WRITE

Write a response to the person you chose in 3A. Give him or her advice, including details and explanations to support your ideas. Remember to use qualifiers. Use the post in 1B as a model.

5 REVISE YOUR WRITING

A PAIRS Exchange posts and read your partner's post.

1. Did you partner include advice?
2. Did your partner include details and explanations to support his or her ideas?
3. Did your partner use qualifiers?

B PAIRS Can your partner improve his or her post? Make suggestions.

6 PROOFREAD

Read your post again. Can you improve your writing?

Check your
- spelling
- punctuation
- capitalization

■ I CAN WRITE ADVICE ON HOW TO MANAGE YOUR TIME.

PUT IT TOGETHER

1 MEDIA PROJECT

▶ **A** ▶ 05-21 Listen or watch. What does Ahmed talk about?

▶ **B** ▶ 05-21 Listen or watch again. Answer the questions.

1. What does Ahmed use the app for? _____
2. What does he like about it? _____
_____
3. How does it help him? _____
_____

C Make your own video.

Step 1 Choose a technology that makes your life or job easier, for example an app or a tool.

Step 2 Make a 30-second video. Talk about how you use it, what you like about it, and how it helps you.

Step 3 Share your video. Answer questions and get feedback.

2 LEARNING STRATEGY

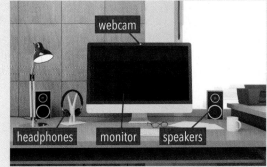

> **LABEL A PICTURE**
>
> Write new vocabulary words on pictures. For example, label the parts of a computer on a picture of a computer. You can do this for all types of words and topics. Writing words on pictures will help you remember the words.

Review the vocabulary words in the unit. What words do you need to learn? Find pictures that represent at least five words or phrases from the unit. Label the pictures. Review the pictures at least once a week.

3 REFLECT AND PLAN

A Look back through the unit. Check (✓) the things you learned. Highlight the things you need to learn.

Speaking objectives
- [ ] Make and respond to suggestions
- [ ] Identify problems and solutions
- [ ] Talk about what you need to do

Vocabulary
- [ ] Technology at work
- [ ] Technology issues and hardware
- [ ] Meeting preparation

Pronunciation
- [ ] Consonant groups
- [ ] Weak and blended pronunciation of *to*

Grammar
- [ ] *Could* and *should* for suggestions
- [ ] *Will*, *may*, and *might* to express likelihood
- [ ] *Have to* / *Need to* for obligation and necessity

Reading
- [ ] Identify text structure: Problem / Solution

Writing
- [ ] Use qualifiers

B What will you do to learn the things you highlighted? For example, use your app, review your Student Book, or do other practice. Make a plan.

Notes   Done

In the app, do the Lesson 2 listening practice: Identify problems and solutions

6 HOW'S YOUR LUNCH?

GET STARTED

A Read the unit title and learning goals.

B Look at the photo of a restaurant. What do you see?

C Now read Sarah's message. What does she mean by "catching up"?

SARAH GOLD
@SarahG

Having lunch with my co-worker today. We haven't talked in a few weeks—looking forward to catching up with her.

SARAH GOLD

@SarahG

If you ask me what my favorite food is, the answer is, everything!

 1 VOCABULARY Adjectives to describe food

A ▶06-01 **Listen. Then listen and repeat.**

| salty | spicy | sweet | bitter | hot |

| cold | strong | weak | sour | rich |

B Complete the sentences with adjectives from 1A.

1. These cookies are very _____ . They must have a lot of sugar in them.
2. This yogurt is _____ . I think it's lemon flavored.
3. My coffee is _____ , so I'm going to put it in the microwave.
4. The soup has a lot of cream in it–it's really _____ .
5. This popcorn is very _____ ! I need something to drink.
6. My tea is too _____ –it's like drinking hot water!

C PAIRS Name one new food for each adjective in 1A.

salty: pretzels; sweet: cookies

 2 GRAMMAR *Too* and *enough* + adjectives

COACH

Too has a negative meaning. It means more than is needed or wanted. *Too* comes before an adjective.

Subject	Verb	*Too*	Adjective
This coffee	is	**too**	**weak.**
The chips	are	**too**	**salty.**

Enough means the right amount. *Not enough* means less than is needed or wanted. *Enough* comes after an adjective.

Subject	Verb	*Not*	Adjective	*Enough*
The soup	is		**spicy**	**enough.**
Those cookies	are	**not**	**sweet**	**enough.**

Note: Infinitives often follow expressions with *too* and *enough*.
*It's not **warm enough to eat**. My coffee is **too hot to drink** right now.*

Use contractions, such as *isn't* or *aren't*, in spoken English and informal writing.

 >> FOR PRACTICE, GO TO PAGE 140

3 PRONUNCIATION

COACH

A ▶06-03 Listen. Notice the different vowel sounds and their spellings. Then listen and repeat.

/i/ e<u>a</u>t sw<u>ee</u>t w<u>ea</u>k   /ɪ/ <u>i</u>t r<u>i</u>ch b<u>i</u>tter

> **The vowels /i/ and /ɪ/**
>
> To say the sound /i/ in <u>eat</u>, pull your lips into a smile. The sound /i/ is a long sound. To say the sound /ɪ/ in <u>it</u>, open your mouth just a little more. The sound /ɪ/ is a shorter and more relaxed sound than /i/.

B ▶06-04 Circle the word in each line that has a different vowel sound. Then listen and check your answers.

1. <u>i</u>s sp<u>i</u>nach del<u>i</u>cious p<u>i</u>zza
2. m<u>ea</u>t br<u>ea</u>d b<u>ea</u>ns ice cr<u>ea</u>m
3. coff<u>ee</u> ch<u>ee</u>se l<u>e</u>mon <u>e</u>vening
4. dr<u>i</u>nk m<u>i</u>lk sp<u>i</u>cy gr<u>i</u>lled

C PAIRS Compare your answers in 3B. Then make 2–3 sentences with the words in 3B.

4 CONVERSATION

A ▶06-05 Listen or watch. Complete the sentences.

1. Sarah is eating a salad with _____ and _____ dressing.
2. When Sarah says the soup is hot, she means that it's very _____ .
3. Sarah likes _____ foods like French fries.
4. They decide to order something _____ after lunch.

B ▶06-06 Listen or watch. Complete the conversation.

> Sarah: How's the curry?
> Alba: It's delicious! But I don't really like the tea. It's _____ bitter.
> Sarah: That's too bad.
> Alba: How do you like the soup?
> Sarah: It's OK, but it's _____ spicy.
> Alba: Really? I don't think it's spicy _____ .

> **CONVERSATION SKILL Show surprise**
>
> You can ask short questions to show that you are surprised by something. To show surprise, ask: (*Oh,) really?*, *It is?*, *They are?*, *Is that right?*, *Oh, yeah?*, or *You do/don't?*
> **A:** This salad is really bitter.
> **B:** Really? I think it tastes good.
> Listen to or watch the conversation in 4A again. Underline the questions that you hear above.

C ▶06-07 Listen and repeat. Then practice with a partner.

D PAIRS Make new conversations. Use the words in 1A or your own ideas.

5 TRY IT YOURSELF

A MAKE IT PERSONAL Think of a time when you had a bad experience with food, at a restaurant or someplace else. For example, was the food too spicy or was it not spicy enough? Take notes.

B PAIRS Discuss your bad experiences. Ask questions to get more information.
   A: I ordered soup for lunch last week and it was too hot!
   B: Is that right? Where were you? What soup did you order?

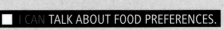

■ I CAN TALK ABOUT FOOD PREFERENCES.

LESSON 2   TALK ABOUT GIFTS

SARAH GOLD
@SarahG

It's great to get gifts, but it's even better to give them.

1 VOCABULARY   Gift items

A ▶06-08 **Listen. Then listen and repeat.**

| roses | chocolates | a necklace | a scarf | a gift card |
| a card | tickets | perfume | cologne | a watch |

B ▶06-09 Listen to the descriptions. Write a gift item from 1A. More than one answer may be possible.

1. _____   3. _____   5. _____

2. _____   4. _____   6. _____

C PAIRS Look at the gift items in 1A. Which would you give to a family member and which would you give to a co-worker? Discuss.

I would give perfume to a family member. I would give a card to a co-worker.

2 GRAMMAR   Verbs + two objects

COACH

Some verbs can have two objects, the direct object and the indirect object. The direct object receives the action of the verb. The indirect object tells who the direct object is for and it often refers to a person.

For some verbs, two different sentence patterns are possible:
subject + verb + indirect object + direct object.
subject + verb + direct object + the preposition *to* or *for* + the indirect object.

Subject	Verb	Indirect object	Direct object
My husband	cooked	me	a wonderful dinner.
I	got	him	a gift card.
My kids	made	me	lots of handmade gifts.

Subject	Verb	Direct object	*For / To*	Indirect object
He	cooked	dinner	for	**Mary**.
My kids	gave	the necklace	to	**me**.

Notes
- Use *to* + the indirect object for these verbs: *bring, give, offer, read, send, show, take, teach, tell, write*
- Use *for* + the indirect object for these verbs: *cook, find, get, make*

>> FOR PRACTICE, GO TO PAGE 141

3 PRONUNCIATION

A ▶06-11 Listen. Notice the pronunciation of the unstressed object pronouns and the linking when *h* is silent. Then listen and repeat.

Ask ~~h~~er.   He gave ~~h~~er a necklace.
Tell ~~h~~im.   She got ~~h~~im a watch.
Call them.   We bought them a card.

> **Weak pronunciation of object pronouns**
>
> Pronouns like *him*, *her*, and *them* are usually unstressed. When *him* and *her* are unstressed, the *h* is often silent. We link the vowel sound after the silent *h* to the word before it: Ask ~~h~~er.

B ▶06-12 Listen. Circle the word you hear. Then listen and repeat.

1. I sent **her** / **him** / **them** an e-mail.
2. We got **her** / **him** / **them** tickets to a show.
3. I gave **her** / **him** / **them** some chocolates.
4. We bought **her** / **him** / **them** a gift card.
5. Did you give **her** / **him** / **them** the gift?
6. I made **her** / **him** / **them** some coffee.

C PAIRS Make 2–3 new sentences like the ones in 3B. Then say the sentences to your partner.

4 CONVERSATION

A ▶06-13 Listen or watch. Circle the correct answers.

1. Alba's children gave her *a necklace* / *perfume* / *a gift card* for Valentine's Day.
2. Sarah's son gave her *chocolates* / *a card* / *cologne*.
3. Sarah got her husband a gift card, but he might also like *a watch* / *cologne* / *chocolates*.
4. Alba is allergic to *perfume* / *strawberries* / *roses*.

B ▶06-14 Listen or watch. Complete the conversation.

Sarah: How was Valentine's Day? Did you get anything special?

Alba: It was good. My boyfriend _____ some roses.

Sarah: Aww. That's sweet. My husband _____ a watch.

Alba: Nice! And what did you get him?

Sarah: I _____ a gift card.

C ▶06-15 Listen and repeat. Then practice with a partner.

D PAIRS Make new conversations. Use the words in 1A or your own ideas.

5 TRY IT YOURSELF

A MAKE IT PERSONAL Think about the best gift you ever got or gave someone. Complete the chart.

Who was it from / for?	What was it?	Why was it the best gift?

B PAIRS Tell your partner about the gift. Explain why it was the best gift.

My mom bought me a necklace. It was the best gift because...

☐ I CAN TALK ABOUT GIFTS.

SARAH GOLD

@SarahG

I love hearing stories about how people met each other.

1 VOCABULARY Storytelling expressions

A ▶06-16 Listen. Then listen and repeat.

eventually: after a long time	**during**: all through a period of time
soon: in a short time from now	**at that moment**: at a point in time
later: after the present time	**meanwhile**: at the same time
as soon as: right after something has happened	**by the time**: not later than the moment that something happened

B Circle the correct answers.

1. We danced a lot **during** / **meanwhile** the party.
2. **As soon as** / **Soon** Ann got to the bus stop, it started to rain.
3. After looking for over an hour, we **eventually** / **later** found the restaurant.
4. **By the time** / **At that moment** he got home, everyone was eating dinner.
5. Tom baked a cake. **Meanwhile** / **Soon**, my Dad was wrapping presents.
6. I couldn't meet with him because I was busy **later** / **at that moment**.

C PAIRS Make sentences using the expressions in 1A.   I fell asleep during the movie.

2 GRAMMAR Past continuous; past continuous with *when*

COACH

Use the past continuous to show an action that was happening at a certain time in the past. The past continuous shows the duration of an action, not its completion.

Affirmative statement			Negative statement			
Subject	**Was / Were**	**Verb + -ing**	**Subject**	**Was / Were**	**Not**	**Verb + -ing**
I	was	**cooking** dinner.	I	was	not	**taking** the train.

Yes / No question			Short answers	
Was / Were	**Subject**	**Verb + -ing**	**Affirmative**	**Negative**
Was	it	**raining**?	Yes, it **was**.	No, it **wasn't**.

Information question				Answer		
Wh- word	**Was / Were**	**Subject**	**Verb + -ing**	**Subject**	**Was / Were**	**Verb + -ing**
What	**were**	you	**watching** yesterday?	I	**was**	**watching** a movie.

Use *when* + the simple past for actions that interrupt the action in the past continuous.

Affirmative statement				
Subject	**Was / Were**	**Verb + -ing**	**When**	**Simple past**
She	**was**	**waiting** to pay	**when**	she **saw** him.

Notes

- Use the simple past, not the past continuous, for actions that were completed without interruptions. *Jim **dropped** his phone and **broke** it.*
- In sentences with *when*, the past continuous shows the action that happened first.
  *Everyone was **eating when** Scott **got** home. = First, they began eating. Then, Scott got home.*

>> FOR PRACTICE, GO TO PAGE 142

3 LISTENING

A ▶06-18 Listen to the story. What is the woman talking about?

a. an interesting trip she took

b. how she met her husband

c. a concert she went to

B ▶06-18 Listen again. Put the events from the story in order. Write the number on the line.

___ a. She went to a concert with her friends, and the man was there.

___ b. She went to the supermarket and saw the man.

___ c. She saw a man with a book she liked.

___ d. They got married.

___ e. They went to dinner and talked for a long time.

___ f. She took the train to work.

C ▶06-18 Read the Listening Skill. Listen again. Listen for the lines below. Circle the emotion that you hear.

1. "I saw someone holding my favorite book, *The Elephant Vanishes*."

   a. surprised   b. angry   c. bored

2. "…all of a sudden I saw the man from the train in the line next to me."

   a. confused   b. tired   c. excited

3. "A few days passed, but I didn't see the 'mystery man' again. To be honest, I was beginning to think I had imagined him!"

   a. worried   b. happy   c. lonely

4. "By the time the concert was over, it was like we had known each other for years."

   a. bored   b. happy   c. confused

> ### LISTENING SKILL
> **Listen for intonation**
>
> Speakers vary the pitch, tone, speed, and volume of their voices to make the things they say more interesting. They also express different emotions such as excitement, surprise, anger, or fear. They may talk slower to emphasize what they are saying, or louder or higher if they are excited, happy, surprised, or angry. As you listen, pay attention to the clues that tell you how the speaker feels.

D PAIRS Compare your answers in 3C. Did you hear the same emotions?

4 TRY IT YOURSELF

A MAKE IT PERSONAL Think about how you met your best friend, boyfriend / girlfriend, husband / wife, or someone important in your life. Take notes.

B PAIRS Tell your partner about how you met this person. Ask questions to get more information.

A: I went to the library to study. As soon as I sat down, a beautiful woman walked in.
B: Really? What happened next?

C WALK AROUND Continue the conversation with your classmates. Take notes in the chart. Report to the class. Who had the most surprising or unusual story?

Who	Where you met	Details

☐ I CAN **TALK ABOUT PAST EVENTS.**

SARAH GOLD
@SarahG

Have you ever eaten dinner while hanging 160 feet above the ground?

1 BEFORE YOU READ

A PAIRS Where is the most interesting or unique restaurant you have ever visited? Discuss.

I once ate at a restaurant under the ocean...

B VOCABULARY ▶06-19 Listen. Then listen and repeat.

| a cave | wildlife | limestone | a cliff | a crane | a platform |

2 READ

>> FOR PRACTICE, GO TO PAGE 156

A PREVIEW Look at the title and photograph. What do you think the article is about?

B ▶06-20 Listen. Read the article.

WHERE ON EARTH?

Restaurants are all about food, right? Well, not always. Sometimes, we go to restaurants because of *where they are*, rather than *what they serve*. Have you ever eaten dinner under the sea? How about in a cave?
5 Or up in the sky? Well, there are restaurants in all of those places!

Under the Sea
Imagine eating dinner in the ocean! There are several underwater restaurants, but the most famous is called
10 Ithaa. It's located in the Maldives, which are islands south of India. The whole restaurant is 16 feet below sea level! The walls and ceiling are made of glass so you can view the ocean's wildlife all around you while you eat! It's been called the "most beautiful restaurant
15 in the world."

In a Cave
What about eating dinner underground? In Polignano a Mare, Italy, there is a restaurant, Grotta Palazzese, that was built inside a cave. The walls of the cave are
20 made of limestone, and the cave is lit by lanterns and candles. The cave is on the side of a cliff right next to the sea, so you can look out over the water as you eat. People have been eating dinner in this cave for hundreds of years! In the 1700s, rich people had
25 special dinners there.

In the Sky
If eating underwater or underground isn't exciting enough, then what about having dinner up in the sky? Really! Dinner in the Sky serves people their meals
30 about 160 feet off of the ground in midair. A dinner table is hung from a crane and raised up into the sky. It's not just a dinner table, though. It's a special platform with room for a chef, a small kitchen, and people to serve the food. Since it first started, Dinner
35 in the Sky has set up special flying dinners all over the world, from Dubai to China.

So, if you're bored with the restaurants in your town, plan a trip to one of these exciting places. You won't even taste the food—you'll be too busy looking around!

People eat dinner 160 feet in the air when they eat at Dinner in the Sky.

3 CHECK YOUR UNDERSTANDING

A Which statement best describes the main idea of the article?

    a. Most restaurants are located in really unique places.

    b. Restaurants located in unique places serve the best food.

    c. It can be fun to eat at restaurants located in unique places.

B Read the article again. Answer the questions.

    1. What might you see when you look out the window at Ithaa? _____

    2. What can people see outside the cave while eating at Grotta Palazzese? _____
    _____

    3. What is raised up in the air during the Dinner in the Sky? _____

    4. What kind of event might have been held at the Grotta Palazzese in the 1700s? _____
    _____

C FOCUS ON LANGUAGE Reread lines 27–36 in the article. Think about the words *Really!* and *set up*. Circle the correct answers.

    1. What does the writer mean by the one-word sentence *Really!*?

        a. I know this sounds strange, but I'm not joking.

        b. I'm not telling you the truth.

        c. I have never heard of anything so silly!

    2. What does the phrase *set up* mean?

        a. made strong

        b. put together

        c. started

> **READING SKILL Construct mental images**
>
> When you read, you should pause to think about what the writer is describing and make a picture in your mind. The writer might include information about what something looks like, where it is, or give you other clues to help you imagine what he or she is describing. This can make the reading easier to understand.

D Read the Reading Skill. Read the article again. What descriptive words does the author use to describe each place? What would you experience if you were there? Complete the chart.

Place	Descriptive words and phrases	What I imagine it would be like

E PAIRS What is the article about? Retell the most important ideas in the article. Use your own words. *The article is about restaurants that are...*

> Find out about other restaurants that are in unique places. 🔍

4 MAKE IT PERSONAL

A Look at the restaurant locations in the chart. Describe what each restaurant would look like, and what it would be like to eat there. Add your own idea for a unique restaurant.

Place	Descriptive words and phrases	What I imagine it would be like
up in a tree		
in an ice cave		

B PAIRS Tell your partner about the restaurant you have imagined.

I think a restaurant in the jungle would be...

■ I CAN READ ABOUT UNIQUE RESTAURANTS.

SARAH GOLD
@SarahG

I just tried a durian, the world's smelliest fruit! It smells so bad, it's not allowed in subways, buses, and hotels!

1 BEFORE YOU WRITE

A What are some strange or unusual foods in your country? Do you like them or not? What are they like?

B Sarah wrote a blog post about an unusual fruit she tried. Why does she think this food is unusual?

► Yesterday's Food Adventure
Home | Discussion Board | Logout

Yesterday, my friend Ava and I were shopping downtown when we came across a strange-looking fruit. It's called a durian. We decided to try one, and we were really surprised.

Both the inside and outside of the fruit look different. The outside is very rough with spikes, but the inside is smooth and thick. Although the appearance of this fruit is very unusual, the strangest thing about it is how it smells and tastes.

Once you open a durian, the smell is very strong. I thought it smelled like old onions! However, I tried a bite anyway. In contrast to the smell, I thought the fruit tasted wonderful! It was rich, a little bit sweet and bitter, and had a flavor of nuts and cheese. Ava, on the other hand, disliked the taste. It wasn't sweet enough for her.

Durian is quite popular in Indonesia, Malaysia, and the Philippines. Personally, I can see why!

Durian is one of the strangest-looking fruits in the world.

C Read the post again. How does Sarah describe the food? What does the food look, smell, and taste like? Take notes in the chart.

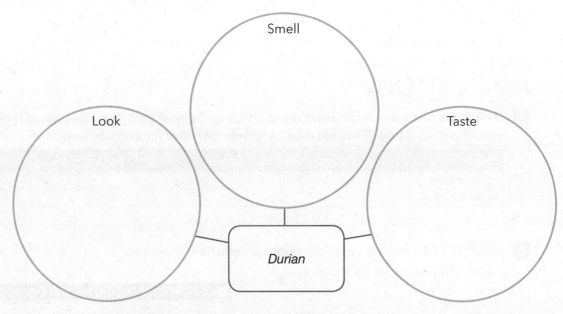

Smell

Look

Taste

Durian

2 FOCUS ON WRITING

A Read the Writing Skill.

B Read the post in 1B again. Underline the words that show contrast.

3 PLAN YOUR WRITING

A Think about the most unusual food you have ever eaten. What made it so unusual? How did it look, smell, and taste? Take notes in the chart.

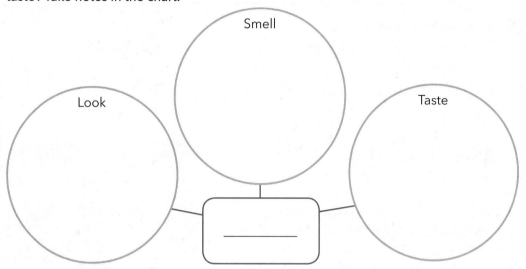

B PAIRS Describe the food to your partner.

The most unusual food I have ever eaten was...

4 WRITE

Write about the food you described in 3A. Describe how the food looked, smelled, and tasted, and why you felt it was unusual. Remember to use words that show contrast. Use the post in 1B as a model.

5 REVISE YOUR WRITING

A PAIRS Exchange posts and read your partner's.
1. Did your partner describe why he or she felt the food was so unusual?
2. Did your partner describe how the food looked, smelled, and tasted?
3. Did your partner use words that show contrast?

B PAIRS Can your partner improve his or her post? Make suggestions.

Check your
• spelling
• punctuation
• capitalization

6 PROOFREAD

Read your post again. Can you improve your writing?

☐ I CAN WRITE ABOUT AN UNUSUAL FOOD.

PUT IT TOGETHER

1 MEDIA PROJECT

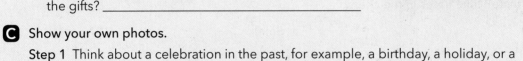

A ▶06-21 Listen or watch. What does Andre talk about?

B ▶06-21 Listen or watch again. Answer the questions.

1. What did they do at the party? _____
2. What food did they have? _____
3. What gifts did Oscar get? _____
4. What's one detail about the food and one detail about the gifts? _____

C Show your own photos.

Step 1 Think about a celebration in the past, for example, a birthday, a holiday, or a graduation party. Choose 3–5 photos that show what you did during the celebration.

Step 2 Show your photos to the class. Talk about the celebration. Describe what you did.

Step 3 Answer questions about your photos. Get feedback on your presentation.

2 LEARNING STRATEGY

> **FIND NEW SOURCES**
>
> Listen to different people speaking English to hear different kinds of intonations and pronunciations. For example, use the Internet to find movies, songs, news, TV shows, and interviews in English. Listen for at least one hour a week.

Listen to the audio or watch the videos from the unit. Pay attention to intonation and pronunciation.

3 REFLECT AND PLAN

A Look back through the unit. Check (✓) the things you learned. Highlight the things you need to learn.

Speaking objectives
- ☐ Talk about food preferences
- ☐ Talk about gifts
- ☐ Talk about past events

Vocabulary
- ☐ Adjectives to describe food
- ☐ Gift items
- ☐ Storytelling expressions

Pronunciation
- ☐ The vowels /i/ and /ɪ/
- ☐ Weak pronunciation of object pronouns

Grammar
- ☐ *Too* and *enough* + adjectives
- ☐ Verbs + two objects
- ☐ Past continuous; past continuous with *when*

Reading
- ☐ Construct mental images

Writing
- ☐ Show contrast

B What will you do to learn the things you highlighted? For example, use your app, review your Student Book, or do other practice. Make a plan.

Notes Done

In the app, listen to Pronunciation 3A
The vowels /i/ and /ɪ/

7 WHERE ARE YOU GOING?

LEARNING GOALS

In this unit, you
- ⊘ talk about an upcoming trip
- ⊘ talk about what you would like to do
- ⊘ talk about geographical features
- ⊘ read about unusual hotels
- ⊘ write a description of a place

GET STARTED

A Read the unit title and learning goals.

B Look at the photo of a vacation. What do you see?

C Now read Mario's message. What does this quote mean?

MARIO CALVO
@MarioC

"Travel is the only thing you buy that makes you richer." – Anonymous

MARIO CALVO
@MarioC

Visiting Mexico City next week.
It's a work trip, but I have some
fun things planned!

1 VOCABULARY Verbs / Adjectives + prepositions

A ▶07-01 **Listen. Then listen and repeat.**

Verbs and adjectives go with specific prepositions. These combinations are often followed by gerunds.

Verb / Adjective	Preposition	Verb / Adjective	Preposition
be excited	about	approve	of
be worried		be afraid	
dream		be fond	
talk		be tired	
think		take care	
apologize	for	adapt	to
be responsible		be used	
blame		feel up	
prepare		look forward	
thank (someone)		object	
be interested	in		
believe			
engage			
participate			
succeed			

B PAIRS Student A, say a verb or adjective from 1A. Student B, say the preposition.

2 GRAMMAR Gerunds as objects of prepositions

COACH

A gerund is a verb + *ing*. It is used the same way as a noun. A gerund is often the object of a preposition.

	Preposition	Object	
I'm interested	**in**	**learning**	more about Mexico City.
She's responsible	**for**	**planning**	the trip.
We look forward	**to**	**hearing**	all about it.
They talked	**about**	**going**	to an unusual restaurant.
He's afraid	**of**	**flying**	too far.

>> FOR PRACTICE, GO TO PAGE 143

3 PRONUNCIATION
COACH

A ▶07-03 Listen. Notice the blended pronunciations of *want to* and *going to*. Then listen and repeat.

going to: I'm going to Mexico City.
/ɡɒnə/: What are you going to do?
/wɑnə/: I want to see the pyramids.

> **Blending: *want to* ("wanna") and *going to* ("gonna")**
>
> We often blend *want to* together as "wanna" /wɑnə/. We often blend *going to* together as "gonna" /ɡɒnə/ when *going to* comes before a verb: *I'm going to leave soon.* We do not blend *going to* together before a noun: *I'm going to Mexico City.*, but *to* is usually unstressed /tə/.

B ▶07-04 Listen. Complete the sentences. Then listen and repeat.

1. _____ Japan in the summer.
2. _____ take cooking classes.
3. _____ learn to make sushi.
4. My friend and _____ go hiking.
5. We're talking about _____ Canada.
6. I think _____ go in August.

C PAIRS Make three sentences with *going to* and *want to* about another idea for a vacation.

4 CONVERSATION

A ▶07-05 Listen or watch. Circle the correct answers.

1. Mario mainly talks about ***a work meeting*** / ***visiting Mexico City*** / ***the Mexican team***.
2. Mario goes to Mexico City ***a few times a year*** / ***every month*** / ***once a year***.
3. Mario hasn't been ***on a hot air balloon tour*** / ***on a private tour*** / ***to a museum***.

B ▶07-06 Listen or watch. Complete the conversation.

Mario: I'm going to Mexico City next week. Have you ever been there?

Eric: No, but I'm interested _____ . What are you going to do?

Mario: We talked _____ to an unusual restaurant. Every dish on the menu includes insects.

Eric: That sounds interesting.

Mario: Yes. I'm excited! We're also going to visit some museums.

Eric: Well, I look forward _____ all about it.

C ▶07-07 Listen and repeat. Then practice with a partner.

D PAIRS Make new conversations. Use these words or your own ideas.
Cancún   the aquarium. They have a lot of unique exhibits.   go ziplining

5 TRY IT YOURSELF

A MAKE IT PERSONAL Think about a place you're planning to visit. Why do you want to visit? What do you want to do there? Take notes.

B PAIRS Talk about the place from 5A. Ask questions to get more information.
  A: I'm interested in visiting Paris. I've never been there.
  B: That's cool. What do you want to do there?

☐ I CAN TALK ABOUT AN UPCOMING TRIP.

TALK ABOUT WHAT YOU WOULD LIKE TO DO

MARIO CALVO
@MarioC

Dreaming of future vacations—where should I go?

1 VOCABULARY Words to describe a place

A ▶07-08 Listen. Then listen and repeat.

clean   polluted

safe   unsafe

ancient   modern

famous   not well known

touristy   unpopular

crowded   deserted

B ▶07-09 Listen to the descriptions. Write one adjective from 1A. More than one answer may be possible.

1. _____   3. _____   5. _____   7. _____
2. _____   4. _____   6. _____   8. _____

C PAIRS Describe a place for your partner using two adjectives from 1A.

London is famous and touristy.

2 GRAMMAR *Would like / love / hate* + infinitive

COACH

Use *would* (*'d*) *like / love / hate* to politely say what you want or don't want. *Would like / love / hate* are followed by an infinitive. Other verbs that are followed by an infinitive include *need, plan,* and *prefer*.

Question				Statements				
Wh-word	Would	Subject	Like	Infinitive	Subject	Would	Not	Like / Love / Hate	Infinitive
What	would	they	like	to do?	They	would	not	love		to a restaurant.
								like	to go	too late.
								hate		someplace crowded.

Notes

- Use *would like, would love,* and *would hate* to talk about possible or imagined events.
  We **would like** / **would love** to go to China someday. I **would hate** to be late for the wedding.
- Use *would like* as a polite way of saying *want* or for offers or requests. Do not use *like, would love,* or *would hate*. **Would** you **like** to join us? **Would** your daughter **like** some ice cream?
- Use the simple present form of *like* to talk about general preferences.
  I **like** to travel to different countries. Ramzy **doesn't like** to wake up early.

>> FOR PRACTICE, GO TO PAGE 144

3 CONVERSATION

 A ▶07-11 Listen or watch. Circle the correct answers.

1. How does Eric describe the "Door to Hell"?
   a. different
   b. touristy
   c. famous
2. What does Mario think about the "Door to Hell"?
   a. He is surprised that Eric wants to go there.
   b. He wants to go there, too.
   c. He thinks lots of people probably go there.
3. Why does Eric want to visit Patagonia soon?
   a. He won't be able to go next year.
   b. He wants to visit before it closes for the season.
   c. He's afraid that it's going to become crowded.

 B ▶07-12 Listen or watch. Complete the conversation.

> Mario: You like to travel, right?
>
> Eric: Yes, I do! I like to visit places that are not well known.
>
> Mario: Really? Like where?
>
> Eric: I'd _____ go to Patagonia.
>
> Mario: Patagonia? Wow. I'd _____ hear more about it.
>
> Eric: OK, sure. But I'm so sorry, I have to go now. I'll tell you more later.

> **CONVERSATION SKILL**
> **End a conversation**
>
> When you want to end a conversation, say: *Well, it was nice talking with you…*, *I've got/I have to go now…*, *I need/have to get going…*, *I should be going now…*, or *I'd love to keep talking with you, but…*
>
> **A:** I need to get going now.
> **B:** Sure. I'll talk to you soon.
>
> Listen to or watch the conversation in 3A again. Underline the expressions that you hear above.

C ▶07-13 Listen and repeat. Then practice with a partner.

D PAIRS Make new conversations. Use these words or your own ideas.

touristy
London

4 TRY IT YOURSELF

A MAKE IT PERSONAL Think about your vacation style. What kinds of places would you like to visit? What's important to you when you travel? What do you like to avoid? Complete the chart.

Kind of place	What's important	What to avoid
famous location	modern, clean, lots of restaurants	unsafe and deserted areas

B PAIRS Talk about your chart in 4A. Describe the kinds of places you would and wouldn't like to visit. Ask questions to get more information.

A: I'd love to visit somewhere famous that's modern and clean.
B: Really? Like where?

■ I CAN TALK ABOUT WHAT I WOULD LIKE TO DO.

MARIO CALVO
@MarioC

What's the hottest place on Earth? The first person who answers gets to take me there on vacation! 😊

1 VOCABULARY Geographical features

A ▶07-14 **Listen. Then listen and repeat.**

| a mountain | a hill | a river | a lake | a pond | an ocean |
| a coast | a forest | an island | a volcano | a desert | a jungle |

B Look at the words in 1A. Write them in the correct category.

Land	Water
a hill	an ocean

C PAIRS Add 2–3 more geographical features to the list in 1A.

2 GRAMMAR Superlative adjectives
COACH

Use superlative adjectives to compare more than two people or things. Use *the* or a possessive adjective (*my / her*, etc.) before the superlative.

Rules	Adjective	Superlative
For most one-syllable adjectives, add *-(e)st* for the superlative.	high large	high**est** large**st**
For one-syllable adjectives ending in one vowel + one consonant, double the final consonant and add *-est*.	hot big	hot**test** big**gest**
For two-syllable adjectives ending in *y*, drop the *y* and add *-iest*.	happy pretty	happ**iest** prett**iest**
For most adjectives with two or more syllables, use *least* or *most* + the adjective.	beautiful popular	**most** beautiful **least** popular

Notes
- Superlatives are often used with prepositional phrases with *in* or *of*.
  *Australia is the **smallest** continent of all.*
- Some adjectives have irregular forms.
  good → **best**   bad → **worst**   far → **farthest / furthest**

>> FOR PRACTICE, GO TO PAGE 145

3 PRONUNCIATION

A ▶07-16 Listen. Notice the way /t/ is dropped before a consonant and linked to a vowel. Then listen and repeat.

the smalles/t country   the largest‿island
the highes/t mountain   the deepest‿ocean

> **Dropping the /t/ and linking in superlatives**
>
> We often drop the sound /t/ in words that end in -st when the next word begins with a consonant sound: *the smalles/t country*. We do this to make a long group of consonant sounds easier to say. When the next word begins with a vowel sound, we pronounce the /t/ and link it to the following vowel: *the largest‿island*.

B ▶07-17 Draw a line (/) through *t* in the superlative if we can drop the sound /t/. Draw a linking line to show where we link *t* to the next word. Listen and check your answers.

1. What's the tallest building?
2. What's the hottest place?
3. What's the most expensive city?
4. Which city has the best food?
5. Which city has the busiest airport?
6. What's the most interesting park?
7. What's the most beautiful city?
8. What's the best time of year to visit?

C PAIRS Ask and answer the questions in 3B about your country.

4 LISTENING

A ▶07-18 Listen to the quiz show. What are the questions about?

a. people   b. numbers   c. places

B ▶07-18 Read the Listening Skill. Listen again. Circle the correct answers.

1. The smallest country in the world has under *100 / 1,000 / 10,000* people.
2. It also has the world's largest *church / palace / park*.
3. The largest lake in the world is in *Asia / Africa / North America*.
4. Aconcagua is more than *22,000 / 28,000 / 32,000* feet tall.
5. The Nile River is *shorter / longer / deeper* than the Yangtze River.
6. The hottest place in the world is *Death Valley / the Sahara Desert / the Australian Outback*.

C PAIRS Compare your answers in 4B.

> **LISTENING SKILL**
> **Listen for specific information**
>
> When you're listening, you don't need to understand every word. Focus on the information you think you'll need in order to understand the topic. For example, listen to places, times, dates, numbers, and names.

5 TRY IT YOURSELF

A MAKE IT PERSONAL Choose three geographical features from 1A. Write three places for each geographical feature. Name places in your country or in other locations. Take notes.

a mountain: Mount Everest, K2, Makalu

B PAIRS Discuss your notes from 5A. Compare the places using adjectives. Which is the highest, smallest / largest, least popular, or most beautiful?

A: For a mountain, I listed Mount Everest, K2, and Makalu.
B: Mount Everest is in China and Nepal. It's the highest mountain in the world.
A: What else do you know about it?

■ I CAN **TALK ABOUT GEOGRAPHICAL FEATURES.**

LESSON 4   READ ABOUT UNUSUAL HOTELS

MARIO CALVO
@MarioC

This hotel not only floats but also turns around in a circle. Now THIS I need to see!

1 BEFORE YOU READ

A PAIRS What kinds of places would you prefer to stay in when you travel?

I prefer to stay at people's houses because...

B VOCABULARY ▶07-19 Listen. Then listen and repeat.

a palace: a large home where a queen or king lives

a rule: a statement of what you can or cannot do

lick: to move the tongue across something

a tank: an object that is used to hold a large amount of a liquid

submerged: under water

rotate: to go around in a circle like a wheel

face: to be towards or in the direction of something

a butler: a person whose job is to serve other people and take care of their home

out of sight: hidden; not able to be seen

>> **FOR PRACTICE, GO TO PAGE 157**

2 READ

A PREVIEW Look at the title and the photograph. What do you think the blog post is about?

B ▶07-20 Listen. Read the blog post.

Blog | About | Destinations | Contact   Search

My World Travels—The Most Interesting Places I've Stayed

When I travel, I try to find interesting places to stay. Here are three of the most beautiful and unique hotels from my travels.

5 The Palacio de Sal (or Palace of Salt) Hotel is truly amazing. It is in the salt desert of Bolivia, at the eastern edge of Salar de Uyuni. What makes this hotel so unique? It is made entirely out of salt! When they first started to build the
10 hotel, building materials were hard to find in the area. But there was plenty of salt. The floor, ceiling, walls, and even some of the furniture are all made of salt. If you're planning a visit, make sure to stay in a room with a view of the desert. It's beautiful. And remember one
15 important rule: Don't lick the walls!

The Marmara Antalya Hotel in Turkey is another great place to visit. Part of this modern hotel is a building that floats in a tank of water. The bottom three floors of this building are
20 completely submerged. The building revolves, or turns in a circle. It is the only hotel in the world that rotates 360 degrees! When I stayed there, I went to sleep facing the pool and woke up facing the sea. I'd love to see those views
25 again! Just remember: Only one building at this hotel turns, so make sure you get a room in the right building.

But there is nowhere more beautiful than the Null Stern Hotel in the Swiss mountains. This hotel is
30 just one "room." The room has a bed, two small tables, two lamps, and nothing else. And I mean nothing else. There are no walls! There is just a bed, outside, surrounded by mountains and sky. A butler stays nearby, but out of sight, and brings
35 guests their meals. The views of the mountains and the star-filled sky are incredible. But be ready to take a walk if you need to go to the bathroom: There isn't one at the hotel. I had to use a public bathroom which was five minutes away!

40 Next week I'll write about the best *free* places I've ever stayed. You'll be surprised by how many there are!

About
RSS Feed
Social Media
Recent Posts
Archives
Email

Leave a reply

Enter your comment here…

THE BEAUTIFUL VIEW FROM MY HOTEL IN THE SALT DESERT.

3 CHECK YOUR UNDERSTANDING

A Which statement best describes the main idea of the blog post?

   a. The best hotels are always unique.

   b. Unique hotels are often expensive.

   c. It is fun to stay in unique hotels.

B Read the blog post again. Circle the correct answers.

   1. Why was the Palacio de Sal made of salt?

      a. It was the best way to attract tourists.

      b. It was hard to find other materials.

      c. It was the cheapest way to build.

   2. What kind of view can you find at the Marmara Antalya Hotel?

      a. the jungle

      b. the desert

      c. the sea

   3. What was one thing the author would have liked at the Null Stern Hotel?

      a. a ceiling

      b. walls

      c. a bathroom

   4. What is one thing all these hotels have in common?

      a. They have great views.

      b. They are in Europe.

      c. They are hard to find.

C FOCUS ON LANGUAGE Reread lines 21-27 in the blog post. Think about the phrases *360 degrees* and *the right building*. Then circle the correct answers.

   1. The expression *360 degrees* means ___ .

      a. a complete circle   b. from left to right   c. halfway around

   2. The phrase *the right building* means ___ .

      a. the building on the right   b. the best building   c. the correct building

D Read the Reading Skill. Look at the blog post in 2B again. Identify the point of view of the author by underlining the pronouns that let you know who is telling the story.

> **READING SKILL** Identify point of view
>
> Identifying the point of view can tell you who is telling the story and how they are telling it. Writers may choose to tell their story in three ways.
>
> First-person: using the pronouns *I* or *we*
>
> Second-person: using the pronoun *you*
>
> Third-person: using the pronouns *he, she, it,* or *they*
>
> Tip: Not every sentence in a story tells you the point of view. To decide which point of view is being used, imagine someone reading the text aloud. Is it a story about themselves or about someone else?

E PAIRS What is the blog post about? Retell the most important ideas in the blog post. Use your own words.

The blog post is about hotels that are...

4 MAKE IT PERSONAL

A GROUPS Think about the blog post you just read. Imagine you are staying in a unique hotel. What makes a hotel an interesting or fun place to stay?

	Details
food	
view	
activities	
services	
other	

🔍 Find out about other unusual places to stay.

B CLASS Report to the class about your ideas.

I would like to stay in a hotel that...

 I CAN READ ABOUT UNUSUAL HOTELS.

LESSON 5 — WRITE A DESCRIPTION OF A PLACE

MARIO CALVO
@MarioC

San Francisco is the best city! Everyone should visit at least once!

1 BEFORE YOU WRITE

A Where is your favorite town or city? What do you like best about it?

B Mario wrote a blog post about San Francisco. What does he think of the city?

Blog | About | Destinations | Contact   🔍 Search

My Favorite City

About
RSS Feed
Social Media
Recent Posts
Archives
Email

Even though I live in Ecuador, I travel a lot for work. San Francisco is one of my favorite places to visit. You should definitely go there!

Most people spend time at touristy places like the Golden Gate Bridge, but I prefer places that are not well known. For example, Corona Heights Park is one of my favorite spots, and it has the most beautiful views of the city.

However, there are a few touristy things to do that are really fun. One of the most interesting places to visit is Alcatraz Island and its famous prison. Don't worry. It's completely safe—the prison is no longer open. It's also nice to walk around Chinatown, eat the wonderful food, and buy some fun souvenirs. The streets are always crowded with people.

If you want to get out of the city, head over to Muir Woods. It is the most amazing forest in the country! The tallest tree in the forest is 258 feet tall and most of the trees are around 500 to 800 years old. Walking in Muir Woods makes me feel better about the world!

There are so many great things to do in San Francisco. Be sure to plan a trip soon!

Leave a reply

Enter your comment here…

Alcatraz Island

Corona Heights Park

Muir Woods

Chinatown

C Read the blog post again. What places does Mario mention? Complete the chart.

Place	Why it's interesting	What you can do there
Corona Heights Park		

2 FOCUS ON WRITING

A Read the Writing Skill.

B Look at the blog post in 1B again. What is the topic of each paragraph?

	Topic
Paragraph 2	
Paragraph 3	
Paragraph 4	

3 PLAN YOUR WRITING

A Think about your hometown or your favorite place to visit. What are the most interesting places to visit there? Complete the chart.

Place	Why it's interesting	What you can do there

B PAIRS Discuss your ideas.

My favorite place to visit is...

4 WRITE

Write a blog post about the places you described in 3A. Describe where a visitor should go, why you recommend the places, and what a person can do there. Remember to include one topic per paragraph. Use the post in 1B as a model.

5 REVISE YOUR WRITING

A PAIRS Exchange posts and read your partner's.

1. Did your partner describe where to go and provide details on why it would be interesting?
2. Did your partner describe what a visitor could do at each place?
3. Did your partner include one topic per paragraph?

B PAIRS Can your partner improve his or her post? Make suggestions.

6 PROOFREAD

Read your post again. Can you improve your writing?

Check your
• spelling
• punctuation
• capitalization

I CAN WRITE A DESCRIPTION OF A PLACE.

PUT IT TOGETHER

1 MEDIA PROJECT

A ▶07-21 Listen or watch. What does Paula talk about?

B ▶07-21 Listen or watch again. Answer the questions.
1. What location is the group going to visit? _____
2. What places does Paula suggest? _____
3. What is one interesting fact about each place? _____

C Show your own photos.

Step 1 Imagine that you are a tour guide, and you are planning a visit for a group of out-of-town visitors. Choose 2–3 photos of places that you think visitors would like to see.

Step 2 Show your photos to the class. Say what the places are and describe them. Give details about why they are interesting.

Step 3 Answer questions about your photos. Get feedback on your presentation.

2 LEARNING STRATEGY

TRAVELING THE WORLD

Are you interested in visiting Bolivia?

LEARN GRAMMAR IN CONTEXT

Study grammar by finding real-life examples of the grammar you're trying to learn, for example, comparative adjectives. You can find grammar examples in books, magazine articles, or on websites. Reviewing grammar in this way will help you to use correct grammar when you're speaking.

Look through travel magazines, books, or websites to find examples of the grammar in this unit. For practice, read the example sentences out loud. Try using the grammar when you speak.

3 REFLECT AND PLAN

A Look back through the unit. Check (✓) the things you learned. Highlight the things you need to learn.

Speaking objectives
- ☐ Talk about an upcoming trip
- ☐ Talk about what you would like to do
- ☐ Talk about geographical features

Grammar
- ☐ Gerunds as objects of prepositions
- ☐ *Would like / love / hate* + infinitive
- ☐ Superlative adjectives

Vocabulary
- ☐ Verbs / Adjectives + Prepositions
- ☐ Words to describe a place
- ☐ Geographical features

Reading
- ☐ Identify point of view

Writing
- ☐ Include one topic per paragraph

Pronunciation
- ☐ Blending: *want to* ("wanna") and *going to* ("gonna")
- ☐ Dropping the /t/ and linking in superlatives

B What will you do to learn the things you highlighted? For example, use your app, review your Student Book, or do other practice. Make a plan.

> Notes   Done
>
> In the app, watch the Lesson 1 conversation; Talk about an upcoming trip
>
> _____
> _____
> _____

8 WHAT ARE YOU DOING TONIGHT?

GET STARTED

A Read the unit title and learning goals.

B Look at the photo of a concert. What do you see?

C Now read Lucas's message. What does his message mean?

LUCAS MORALES
@LucasM

Traveling this week for work.
Hope to get out for some fun.

LUCAS MORALES
@LucasM

I love listening to music! I have a song for every part of my day.

 1 VOCABULARY Instruments and musicians

A ▶08-01 **Listen. Then listen and repeat.**

| a guitar / a guitarist | a piano / a pianist | drums / a drummer | a bass / a bassist |

| a keyboard / a keyboardist | a trumpet / a trumpeter | a saxophone / a saxophonist | a violin / a violinist |

B ▶08-02 **Listen. What do you hear? Who is playing the instrument? Number the images in 1A.**

C PAIRS **Cover the words in 1A. Test your partner. Student A, say an instrument. Student B, say the word for the musician. Keep score.**

A: a trumpet
B: a trumpeter

 2 GRAMMAR Questions about the subject and object

COACH

In questions about the subject, the *wh-* word is the subject of the verb. The answer tells us the subject.

Questions about the subject			Answers
Wh- word	Main verb	Object	
Who	is	the guitarist?	**Joe** is the guitarist.
What	happened	this weekend?	**A band** performed at the park.
Which band	sings	this song?	**Talking Hearts** sings this song.

In questions about the object, the *wh-* word is the object of the verb. The answer tells us the object.

Questions about the object				Answers
Wh- word	Auxiliary verb	Subject	Main verb	
Who	are	you	listening to?	I'm listening to **Talking Hearts.**
What	is	she	playing?	She's playing **the piano**.

Note: Most questions about the subject use *who* or *what*. There is no auxiliary verb.
For questions about the object, an auxiliary verb comes before the subject.

>> FOR PRACTICE, GO TO PAGE 146

3 PRONUNCIATION

COACH

A ▶08-04 Listen. Notice the different intonations. Then listen and repeat.

Wonderful! You're kidding! That's great!
Wonderful! You're kidding! That's great!

> **Intonation: Showing enthusiasm**
>
> When someone is showing enthusiasm or strong interest, their intonation often goes up very high and then goes down. If your intonation is too low or too flat, it can sound like you're not interested or you mean the opposite of what you're saying.

B ▶08-05 Listen to the intonation in speaker B's response. Which sentence do you think speaker A said? Circle the correct answers. Then listen and check your answers.

1. a. I got the job.
   b. The computers are all down.
2. a. I got free tickets to see Lady Gaga.
   b. Our flight was canceled.
3. a. Sam and I are getting married.
   b. We're going to miss the train.
4. a. I'm going to France next year.
   b. It's raining again.

C PAIRS Use the responses in 3A. Create two dialogs, one showing enthusiasm and the other showing a lack of enthusiasm.

4 CONVERSATION

A ▶08-06 Listen or watch. Circle the correct answers.

1. Mandy is surprised Lucas knows Talking Hearts because they're **not well known** / **from Canada** / **a new band**.
2. Talking Hearts have just **made an album** / **finished touring** / **visited Vancouver**.
3. The Clouds are from **Canada** / **the U.K.** / **South America**.
4. Emma Taylor plays the **guitar and drums** / **bass and trumpet** / **drums and piano**.

B ▶08-07 Listen or watch. Complete the conversation.

Lucas: _____ you listening to?

Mandy: A band called Talking Hearts. Here. Listen.

Lucas: Cool. I like this song. I love the guitar solo.

Mandy: Yeah. Me, too. It's amazing.

Lucas: _____ the guitarist?

Mandy: His name is Joe Ramos.

C ▶08-08 Listen and repeat. Then practice with a partner.

D PAIRS Make new conversations. Use the words in 1A or your own ideas.

5 TRY IT YOURSELF

A MAKE IT PERSONAL Think of a popular song. Think about the members of the band or artist and the instruments they play. Take notes.

B GAME Student A, sing a few lines of the song in 5A. Student B, ask questions about the song and the band. Try to guess the song.

B: Who sings this song?
A: The band is called Maná.

■ I CAN TALK ABOUT MUSIC.

LUCAS MORALES
@LucasM

I just learned my favorite band is on tour. I'd really love to see a show!

1 VOCABULARY Evening events

A ▶08-09 Listen. Then listen and repeat.

see a show

go to an art gallery

go to a game

see a musical

go to a comedy club

see a movie

go to the opera

go to the ballet

B ▶08-10 Listen to the sentences. Write the correct activity from 1A.

1. _____   3. _____   5. _____

2. _____   4. _____   6. _____

C PAIRS Take turns describing an activity from 1A that you like to do.

I like to go to comedy clubs. I love to laugh.

2 GRAMMAR So / Because (of) to show cause and effect

Use *so* to introduce an effect, or a result of something.

Cause / Reason	So	Effect / Result
It isn't a famous band,	**so**	I'm sure we can still get tickets.
My boyfriend loves them,	**so**	he'll probably want to come with us.

Note: *So* goes between two independent clauses. A comma usually comes immediately before *so*.

Use *because* and *because of* to introduce the cause of a cause-and-effect relationship.

Because / Because of	Cause / Reason	Effect / Result
Because	it's near the club,	let's eat at Pasha Café.
Because of	the traffic,	we're going to be late.

Notes
- *Because* or *because of* can go at the beginning or the middle of the sentence.
  Because *I'm meeting some friends, I can't go. I can't go* **because** *I'm meeting some friends.*
- *Because* is followed by a subject and a verb. *Because of* is followed by a noun or noun phrase.
- When *because* or *because of* comes first in the sentence, the phrase or clause is followed by a comma. When the main clause comes first, there is no comma.

>> FOR PRACTICE, GO TO PAGE 147

3 PRONUNCIATION

COACH

A ▶08-12 Listen. Notice the way speaker B uses main stress to emphasize a different word for contrast in each conversation. Then listen and repeat.

1. A: Are you free on Thursday at 10?
   B: No, how about **Friday** at 10?

2. A: Are you free on Friday at 8?
   B: No, how about Friday at 10?

B ▶08-13 The main stress is underlined for Speaker A. Underline the word that should have the main stress in Speaker B's response. Then listen and check your answers.

1. A: I think the show starts at 8:<u>30</u>.
   B: No, actually, it starts at 9:30.

2. A: Let's meet at the restaurant at <u>7</u>.
   B: Could we make that 7:15?

3. A: The drummer is <u>British</u>, right?
   B: No, the guitarist is British.

4. A: Should I buy a <u>ticket</u> for you?
   B: Thanks, but I already have a ticket.

C PAIRS Practice the short conversations in 3B. Then make similar conversations.

4 CONVERSATION

A ▶08-14 Listen or watch. Circle the correct answers.

1. Lucas is in town until **Thursday** / **Friday** / **Saturday**.
2. The tickets should be **easy to get** / **expensive** / **cheap**.
3. Lucas asks Mandy to **lend him money** / **buy the tickets** / **get him some cash**.
4. On Friday, Lucas is going to **an art gallery** / **a game** / **a show**.

B ▶08-15 Listen or watch. Complete the conversation.

Mandy: Do you want to see a show on Wednesday?

Lucas: I'd love to, but I can't _____ I'm meeting some friends.

Mandy: Oh, OK. There's another one on Thursday night. Are you free?

Lucas: Yes, I am.

Mandy: Great. They just added this show, _____ I'm sure we can still get tickets.

Lucas: Sounds good. I'm in.

C ▶08-16 Listen and repeat. Then practice with a partner.

D PAIRS Make new conversations. Use these words or your own ideas.

see a movie
showtime

5 TRY IT YOURSELF

ROLE PLAY Make plans with your partner for an evening activity. Decline the invitation, and make another suggestion.

A: Do you want to get together on Friday night?
B: I'm sorry, but I can't because I have plans. How about Saturday evening?

■ I CAN TALK ABOUT EVENING PLANS.

LESSON 3   DESCRIBE HABITS AND ROUTINES

LUCAS MORALES
@LucasM

If you've been looking for an easy way to get healthy, you're in luck—sleeping counts!

1 VOCABULARY Healthy habits

A ▶08-17 Listen. Then listen and repeat.

get a check-up

go for a run

go to the gym

spend time outdoors

meditate

get enough sleep

cut down on sugar

follow a balanced diet

put down your device

drink water

B Look at the healthy habits in 1A. Put them into the groups.

Rest	Exercise	Diet	Other

C PAIRS Talk about a habit from 1A that you don't do but would like to do. How can you make it happen?

I'd like to drink more water. I can fill up a large bottle with water in the morning.

2 GRAMMAR Time expressions

Use time expressions with the simple present tense to talk about things that happen often, regularly, or all the time.

I go swimming	**every day.**	I use my device	**once an hour.**
I meditate	**every morning.**	I go to the gym	**twice a week.**
I go for a run	**on Mondays.**	I go for a hike	**three times a month.**
I spend time outdoors	**on weekends.**	I get a check-up	**a few times a year.**

Notes
- Time expressions made up of two or more words can go either at the beginning or the end of a sentence. When a time expression comes at the beginning of the sentence, it is sometimes followed by a comma.
  *Leah goes to the gym **every Monday**.   **Every Monday**, Leah goes to the gym.*
- Add -ly to words like *day* and *night* to show something happens every day or every night.
  *Maya exercises every night. = Maya exercises **nightly**.*
  *Her blog comes out every day. = Her blog comes out **daily**.*
  Other common examples include *hourly, weekly, monthly, quarterly,* and *yearly*.

>> FOR PRACTICE, GO TO PAGE 148

3 LISTENING

A ▶08-19 Listen to the podcast. What is the woman talking about?

    a. new ways of using technology to get healthy

    b. problems from using technology too much

    c. how many hours a week people use their devices

B ▶08-19 Read the Listening Skill. Listen again for example phrases. Circle the answers that are mentioned in the audio. Each question has two correct answers.

1. People aren't getting enough sleep.
   a. People go to bed with their devices.
   b. The light from our devices keeps us awake.
   c. People wake up early to use their devices.
2. Too much screen time can change a part of the brain.
   a. Kids may not learn how to have good relationships with people.
   b. Adults may forget how to have relationships.
   c. Adults may have friends online, but not in real life.
3. Instead of picking up your device, try something new.
   a. Start a new hobby.   b. Play a new game online.   c. Take a class.
4. Spend time with family and friends.
   a. Have dinner together.
   b. Catch up with each other.
   c. Socialize by chatting online.
5. Do something for yourself.
   a. Do some online shopping.
   b. Find some quiet time.
   c. Focus on yourself for part of the day.

> **LISTENING SKILL** Listen for examples and supporting statements
>
> Speakers use certain phrases to introduce examples and supporting statements. These help to support speakers' ideas so that listeners understand them better. Some common phrases are: *such as, like, for example / for instance, for one thing / for another thing, in fact, in general, in particular / in detail,* and *let me explain.*

C ▶08-19 Listen again. Complete the sentences.

The Effects of Too Much Screen Time	
Problems	**Solutions**
People aren't getting enough sleep.	Stop using your device at least (1) _____ before bed-time so you can start to (2) _____ .
Too much screen time can change a part of the brain that helps people (3) _____ and build relationships.	Parents should (4) _____ their own screen time, as well as their kids'.

D PAIRS Compare your answers in 3C. Did you get the same answers?

4 TRY IT YOURSELF

A MAKE IT PERSONAL Think about your weekly routine. What are your good and bad habits? What bad habits would you like to change? Take notes.

B PAIRS Discuss your habits. Ask questions to get more information.

    A: I go to school five days a week. It's hard to find time to exercise.

    B: What do you do on the weekends?

    A: I like to spend time outdoors.

    B: Maybe you could try…

■ I CAN DESCRIBE HABITS AND ROUTINES.

LUCAS MORALES

@LucasM

Ever wonder why loud music makes you feel good? Scientists have the answer.

1 BEFORE YOU READ

A   PAIRS   Discuss. What kind of music do you like? Say why.

I really love...

B   VOCABULARY   ▶08-20 Listen. Then listen and repeat.

> **a mood**: the way a person feels at a certain time
> **stress**: a feeling of worry that stops a person from being able to relax
> **a rhythm**: a regular, repeated pattern of sounds
> **beat**: to make a regular movement or sound
> **translate**: to change something into another form
> **heart rate**: the number of times the heart beats in a minute
> **a piece**: something that someone has made, written, or drawn
> **a hormone**: something the body makes that helps you to grow and change
> **release**: to let something go into the body, air, water, soil, etc.

>> FOR PRACTICE, GO TO PAGE 157

2 READ

A   Read the Reading Skill.

B   ▶08-21 Listen. Read the article. As you read, stop and ask yourself these questions. *Do I understand what I just read? Do I need to reread anything? Do I need to look up any words?*

> **READING SKILL**
>
> **Ask and answer questions**
>
> Asking questions while you read helps you understand the text. As you read, stop and ask questions about the text. Do you understand what you are reading? Do you need to look up any words?

The **Power** of Music

We all know that music affects our moods. It can make us feel great joy or make us think of our saddest moments. Soft music can calm an upset baby. And singing along to loud music can help someone get rid of stress or anger. But why? Why does music have this powerful effect?

Scientists have learned that music affects both our bodies and brains. Our hearts
5   beat at the same speed as the rhythms we hear. For example, fast music makes our hearts beat faster and slow music makes our hearts beat more slowly. Our brains translate these different heart rates into emotions. So, a loud, fast rock song can make us feel like we have more energy, and a slow, classical violin piece can make us feel calmer and less stressed.

10   Music also affects the hormones in our bodies. Studies have shown that when we listen to slow, quiet music, our bodies produce fewer stress hormones and more of the hormones that make us feel happy. But it's not only calm, quiet music that makes us feel good. Loud, fast music can move a small part of the ear which then tells the brain to release endorphins.
15   Endorphins can make us feel positive and happy. More endorphins are released at higher volume levels. The louder the music, the higher the level of endorphins.

Music affects us in many ways.

Other studies have shown that listening to almost any kind of music can help people who suffer from short-term pain, such as a large cut or burn, or from a long-term illness, such as heart disease.

20 Music can help in two ways: It can trigger the release of endorphins which, in addition to making us feel happy, can also reduce our pain levels. And, more simply, it can help us to think about something other than the pain we are feeling. However, scientists do believe that we have to like the music in order for it to have a positive effect.

So, the next time you're sad and you want to feel happy, or you're in pain and you want to feel better,
25 listen to your favorite song. Music really *can* help you feel better. Now *that's* music to your ears!

3 CHECK YOUR UNDERSTANDING

A Which statement best describes the main idea of the article?
   a. Music can have a powerful effect on our bodies and minds.
   b. The best way to relax and have a good time is to listen to music.
   c. Slow, quiet music is the only kind of music that can help people who are upset.

B Read the article again. Circle the correct answers.
   1. Our hearts beat ___ the sounds we hear.
      a. faster than   b. slower than   c. at the same speed as
   2. The brain produces ___ when we listen to slow music.
      a. fewer stress hormones   b. more stress hormones   c. fewer positive hormones
   3. ___ music moves a part of the ear which tells the brain to release endorphins.
      a. Loud and slow   b. Loud and fast   c. Soft and slow
   4. Someone who is in pain should listen to ___ .
      a. their favorite song   b. any kind of music   c. nothing at all

C FOCUS ON LANGUAGE Reread lines 20-25 in the article. Think about the words *trigger* and *that's music to your ears*. Then circle the correct answers.
   1. In this sentence, the word *trigger* means ___ .
      a. part of a gun   b. to make something happen   c. to move something with a finger
   2. The expression *that's music to your ears* means ___ .
      a. that's a great song   b. that's good news   c. that's terrible news

D PAIRS What is the article about? Retell the most important ideas in the article. Use your own words.
   The article is about how music...

Find out about other ways music affects people. 🔍

4 MAKE IT PERSONAL

A Think about the article you just read. Answer the questions.
   1. Do you agree or disagree with the author of the article?
      _____
      _____
   2. Did you learn something new? What did you learn?
      _____
      _____

B PAIRS Discuss your answers in 4A.
   I agree with the author. I think...

☐ I CAN READ ABOUT THE POWER OF MUSIC.

LESSON 5   WRITE SUGGESTIONS FOR MEETING PEOPLE

LUCAS MORALES
@LucasM

You know who makes new friends the easiest? Pet owners. Everyone stops to talk to you when you have a dog. 😊

1 BEFORE YOU WRITE

A What do you like to do after work or on weekends? Is it a good way to meet new people?

B Charlie posted a question on a discussion board. Lucas replied with some suggestions. Read the posts. What question does Charlie ask?

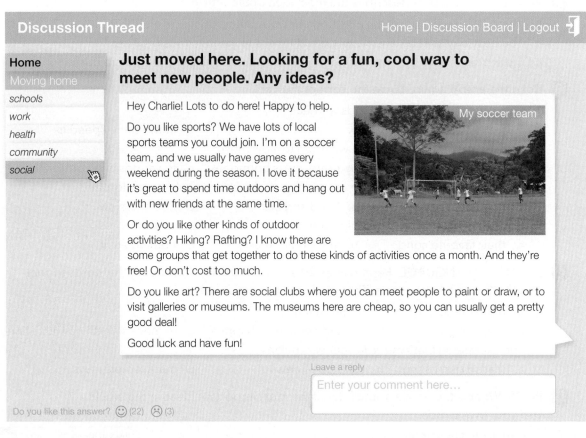

Discussion Thread   Home | Discussion Board | Logout

Home
Moving home
schools
work
health
community
social

Just moved here. Looking for a fun, cool way to meet new people. Any ideas?

Hey Charlie! Lots to do here! Happy to help.

Do you like sports? We have lots of local sports teams you could join. I'm on a soccer team, and we usually have games every weekend during the season. I love it because it's great to spend time outdoors and hang out with new friends at the same time.

My soccer team

Or do you like other kinds of outdoor activities? Hiking? Rafting? I know there are some groups that get together to do these kinds of activities once a month. And they're free! Or don't cost too much.

Do you like art? There are social clubs where you can meet people to paint or draw, or to visit galleries or museums. The museums here are cheap, so you can usually get a pretty good deal!

Good luck and have fun!

Leave a reply

Enter your comment here...

Do you like this answer? 😊 (22) 😞 (3)

C Read the posts again. What does Lucas suggest to Charlie? Take notes in the chart.

	Idea	Details
Suggestion 1		
Suggestion 2		
Suggestion 3		

2 FOCUS ON WRITING

A Read the Writing Skill.

WRITING SKILL **Write informally**
Informal writing is similar to spoken conversation, and it follows fewer grammar rules than formal writing. We often use incomplete sentences in informal writing. Contractions (*I'm, doesn't, couldn't, it's*) and abbreviations (*TV, photos*) are also used. Formal writing: *It was a pleasure to meet you yesterday. I hope we can see each other again very soon.* Informal writing: *Great to meet you! Hope to see you again soon.*

B Reread the discussion board posts. Underline the incomplete sentences.

3 PLAN YOUR WRITING

A Think about Charlie's question. How could someone meet new people in your town? Complete the chart.

	Idea	Details
Suggestion 1		
Suggestion 2		
Suggestion 3		

B PAIRS Describe your suggestions to your partner.

I think someone who wants to meet new people could…

4 WRITE

Imagine you are answering Charlie's question. What things would you suggest he do to meet new people in your town? Use your suggestions from 3A. Remember to use informal writing. Use the post in 1B as a model.

5 REVISE YOUR WRITING

A PAIRS Exchange posts and read your partner's.
1. Did you partner include suggestions in his or her post?
2. Did your partner use informal writing in his or her post?

B PAIRS Can your partner improve his or her post? Make suggestions.

Check your
• spelling
• punctuation
• capitalization

6 PROOFREAD

Read your post again. Can you improve your writing?

I CAN **WRITE SUGGESTIONS FOR MEETING PEOPLE.**

PUT IT TOGETHER

1 MEDIA PROJECT

▶ **A** ▶08-22 Listen or watch. What does Rina talk about?

▶ **B** ▶08-22 Listen or watch again. Answer the questions.

1. What are Rina's healthy habits? _____
2. How often does she do these activities? _____
   _____
3. Why does she do these activities? Write one reason.
   _____

C Share your own photos.

Step 1 Think about your healthy habits, or things you do to stay healthy, happy, or relaxed. Think about how often you do these activities and why you do them.

Step 2 Show your photos to the class. Talk about your healthy habits. Say why you do these activities and how often you do them.

Step 3 Answer questions about your photos. Get feedback on your presentation.

2 LEARNING STRATEGY

> **CREATE CONNECTIONS**
>
> Connect new words with ones you already know. Make flashcards of sentences using the new words with blanks for words you already know. Write words for the blanks on the back of the card. For example, *I go to the ballet because I love the _____*, can be completed with *music, dancing,* or *costumes.*

I go to the ballet because I love the
_____.

music/dancing/
costumes

Review the vocabulary in the unit. What words do you need to learn? Make five flashcards with the words. Be sure to have sentences with blanks and connected words for each flashcard. Review the cards twice a week.

3 REFLECT AND PLAN

A Look back through the unit. Check (✓) the things you learned. Highlight the things you need to learn.

Speaking objectives
- ☐ Talk about music
- ☐ Talk about evening plans
- ☐ Describe habits and routines

Vocabulary
- ☐ Instruments and musicians
- ☐ Evening events
- ☐ Healthy habits

Pronunciation
- ☐ Intonation: Showing enthusiasm
- ☐ Main stress to emphasize a contrast

Grammar
- ☐ Questions about the subject and object
- ☐ So / Because (of) to show cause and effect
- ☐ Time expressions

Reading
- ☐ Ask and answer questions

Writing
- ☐ Write informally

B What will you do to learn the things you highlighted? For example, use your app, review your Student Book, or do other practice. Make a plan.

Notes — Done

Do the Learning Strategy: Create connections, page 100.

_____
_____
_____

9 WHERE DO YOU WANT TO MEET?

LEARNING GOALS

In this unit, you
⊘ talk about plans
⊘ talk about reasons for being late
⊘ talk about where things are
⊘ read product reviews
⊘ write about your dream home

GET STARTED

A Read the unit title and learning goals.

B Look at the photo of people moving. What do you see?

C Now read Alba's message. What does her message mean?

ALBA PARDO
@AlbaP

It's going to be a busy week—
my whole calendar is filled!

ALBA PARDO
@AlbaP

Love this quote! "A goal without a plan is just a wish."
– Antoine de Saint-Exupéry

1 VOCABULARY Living room furniture and decor

A ▶09-01 Listen. Then listen and repeat.

curtains · a frame · a painting · a coffee table · a carpet · a couch · an end table

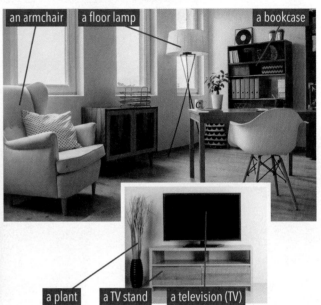

an armchair · a floor lamp · a bookcase · a plant · a TV stand · a television (TV)

B ▶09-02 Listen to the conversation. Circle the things that will go in the living room.

a bookcase   an end table   a couch   a TV stand   an armchair

C PAIRS Describe your living room using the words from 1A. Say 2-3 sentences.

I have a green couch in my living room. There are two small armchairs.

2 GRAMMAR Future with *will, be going to,* present continuous, and simple present

COACH

Use *will* + the base form of the verb for predictions, offers, and quick decisions made at the moment of speaking.

Predictions	We're all excited about the project. I think tomorrow's meeting **will be** great.
Offers	Those boxes look heavy. We**'ll help** you carry them.
Quick decisions	That's a great price. I**'ll take** it!

Use *be going to* + the base form of the verb for predictions and to talk about specific plans.

| Predictions | Bob just got a new apartment, and he**'s going to need** a lot of furniture. |
| Specific plans | We need a lot of furniture. We**'re going to go** shopping this weekend. |

Use the present continuous to talk about specific plans.

| Specific plans | I can't wait for the weekend. We**'re having** dinner with my cousins from Lima. |

Use the simple present for future events that are on a definite schedule, such as store hours, bus and train schedules, flight times, and movie showings.

| Definite schedules | His flight **gets** in at 9:00 on Sunday. |

>> FOR PRACTICE, GO TO PAGE 149

3 CONVERSATION

 A ▶09-04 Listen or watch. Circle the correct answers.

1. What is happening on Monday afternoon?
   a. Alba and Teo are going to a meeting.
   b. Alba is going to buy furniture.
   c. Teo is meeting Mario.
2. What is happening with Alba's cousin?
   a. She is moving overseas.
   b. She just started a new job.
   c. Her apartment flooded.
3. What furniture does Alba's cousin *not* need?
   a. a floor lamp and an armchair
   b. a coffee table and a TV stand
   c. a bookcase and an end table
4. Why does Teo suggest that they meet his friend to look at furniture?
   a. to help Alba out
   b. to save her cousin some money
   c. to help his friend sell some furniture

 B ▶09-05 Listen or watch. Complete the conversation.

> Alba: I'm _____ furniture shopping with my cousin this weekend.
>
> Teo: Oh yeah? What does she need?
>
> Alba: She needs a couch, a bookcase, and a table.
>
> Teo: My friend _____ some of his furniture. Do you want to take a look?
>
> Alba: That's a great idea!
>
> Teo: I think _____ around this weekend. _____ a call.
>
> Alba: Perfect. Thanks so much.

C ▶09-06 Listen and repeat. Then practice with a partner.

D PAIRS Make new conversations. Use the words in 1A or your own ideas.

4 TRY IT YOURSELF

A MAKE IT PERSONAL Think about the furniture in your home. Think of something you need or that you'd like to buy for a specific room. Take notes.

B PAIRS Tell your partner about the furniture you're going to buy. Make plans to go shopping.

A: I'm going to buy a floor lamp for my bedroom. The one I have doesn't work anymore.
B: OK. Let's go shopping tomorrow morning. Where should we go?
A: The furniture store is having a sale.
B: Sounds good. I'll meet you there at 10:00.

■ I CAN TALK ABOUT PLANS.

ALBA PARDO
@AlbaP

The trouble with being on time is that no one is there to appreciate it. 😂

 1 VOCABULARY Reasons for being late

A ▶09-07 Listen. Then listen and repeat.

 I had to work late.

 I got stuck in traffic.

 My car broke down.

 My train was delayed.

 I lost my keys.

 I got lost.

 I got stuck in bad weather.

 I had an accident.

 I overslept.

 I missed the bus.

B ▶09-08 Listen to the sentences. Write the correct reason for being late from 1A.

1. _____   4. _____
2. _____   5. _____
3. _____   6. _____

C PAIRS Brainstorm. Think of three more reasons for being late.

2 GRAMMAR Indirect questions
COACH

Use indirect questions to be polite or if you're not sure the person will know the answer to the question.

Direct *wh-* questions					Indirect questions			
Wh- word	Auxiliary verb	Subject	Main verb			*Wh-* word	Subject	Verb
Where	**is**	he?			I wonder	where	he	**is**.
Why	**isn't**	she	**answering**?		I don't know	why	she	**isn't answering**.
When	**did**	you	**plan** to leave?		Can you tell me	when	you	**planned** to leave?

In *yes / no* questions, use *if* or *whether* before the subject.

Direct *yes / no* questions				*If / Whether*	Subject	Verb
Auxiliary verb	Subject	Main verb				
Is	he	**here** yet?	Do you know	**if**	he	**is here** yet?
Were	they	**late**?	Can you tell me	**whether**	they	**were late**?

Notes
- Indirect questions often appear after introductory phrases, such as *I wonder, I don't know, Can / Could you tell me, Do you know, I'd like to know,* or *Would you mind explaining*.
- We always use statement word order in indirect questions. The subject always comes before the verb.

>> FOR PRACTICE, GO TO PAGE 150

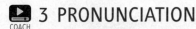

3 PRONUNCIATION

A ▶09-10 Listen. Notice the different vowel sounds spelled by the letter *a*. Then listen and repeat.

/eɪ/	/æ/	/ɑ/	/ə/
l<u>a</u>te	c<u>a</u>b	c<u>a</u>r	<u>a</u>ddress

The letter *a*

In stressed syllables and words with one syllable, the letter *a* usually has the sound /eɪ/ (*l<u>a</u>te*) or /æ/ (*c<u>a</u>b*). When the letter *a* comes before *r*, however, it usually has the sound /ɑ/ (*c<u>a</u>r*). In unstressed syllables, the letter *a* often has the sound /ə/ (*<u>a</u>ddress*).

B ▶09-11 Write each word in the correct column in 3A. Then listen and check your answers.

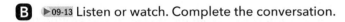

sof<u>a</u>   tr<u>a</u>ffic   tr<u>a</u>in   b<u>a</u>d   <u>a</u>rmchair
t<u>a</u>ble   <u>a</u>ccident   <u>a</u>partment   <u>a</u>rtwork   del<u>a</u>yed

C PAIRS Add one more word to each column in 3A.

4 CONVERSATION

A ▶09-12 Listen or watch. Circle the correct answers.
1. Mario **missed the bus** / **overslept** / **lost his keys**.
2. The cab driver **got stuck in traffic** / **went to the wrong address** / **got stuck in bad weather**.
3. Mario couldn't call for help because he **lost his phone** / **forgot his phone** / **forgot Alba's number**.

B ▶09-13 Listen or watch. Complete the conversation.

> **Teo:** You look worried. Is everything OK?
> **Alba:** I'm just worried about Mario. I wonder _____ .
> **Teo:** I'm sure he's OK. Maybe he overslept.
> **Alba:** I don't think so. Maybe he got lost, or maybe he is stuck in traffic.
> **Teo:** Could be. Does he know _____ ?
> **Alba:** Yes, he knows where it is. I'm going to call him.

CONVERSATION SKILL
Ask if there is a problem

If you want to ask someone if he or she is having a problem, say: *Is everything OK?, Are you all right?, Is there a problem?, Is something the matter?,* or *What's wrong?*
A: What's wrong?
B: My friend is really late!
Listen to or watch the conversation in 4A again. Underline the questions that you hear above.

C ▶09-14 Listen and repeat. Then practice with a partner.

D PAIRS Make new conversations. Use these words or your own ideas.

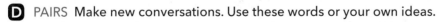

his car broke down
lost his keys
stuck in bad weather

5 TRY IT YOURSELF

A MAKE IT PERSONAL Think about a time you were late. When did it happen? What happened and why? What did you do? Take notes.

B PAIRS Tell your partner about the time you were late. Ask questions.
A: I was late for my first day at work.
B: Oh, no. What happened?
A: I lost my keys and I didn't know where they were. So I...

☐ I CAN TALK ABOUT REASONS FOR BEING LATE.

ALBA PARDO
@AlbaP

I'm always losing things in my house! I'd lose my head if it weren't attached to my body.

 1 VOCABULARY Places in and around the house

A ▶09-15 Listen. Then listen and repeat.

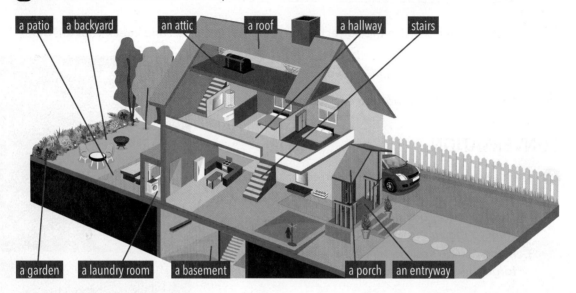

a patio | a backyard | an attic | a roof | a hallway | stairs

a garden | a laundry room | a basement | a porch | an entryway

B Draw a diagram of your house or a house you know. Label the places in and around the house using the words from 1A.

C PAIRS Student A, describe the house from 1B. Student B, draw a diagram of your partner's house. Then check your partner's diagram.

A: There's a laundry room in the basement.
B: OK. And what's on the main floor?

 2 GRAMMAR Adverbs and adverbial phrases of place
COACH

Adverbs and adverbial phrases of place tell us *where* something happens. They usually go at the end of a sentence.

	Adverb		Adverbial phrase
Let's eat	**outside.**	There's a table	**on the patio.**
The cat is	**upstairs.**	It's sleeping	**in my room.**
The kids are playing	**nearby.**	They're	**at the neighbor's house.**

Here are some common adverbial phrases.

in	the middle, the front, the back, the world, the city, the country, the house, the backyard, the kitchen, the building
on	the street, the ground, the floor, the patio, the table, the shelf
at	home, work, the office, school, the library

Note: It's possible to use more than one adverb or adverbial phrase in a sentence.
*John is **outside in the garden**.   I left my books **somewhere at school**.*

>> FOR PRACTICE, GO TO PAGE 151

3 PRONUNCIATION

A ▶09-17 Listen. Notice the stress in the compounds. Then listen and repeat.

bo͏̇okcase, li͏̇ving room: There's a bo͏̇okcase in the li͏̇ving room.

e͏̇verything: Is e͏̇verything OK?

inside: Let's go insi͏̇de.

B ▶09-18 Underline the two compounds in each sentence. Put a dot over the stressed syllable in each compound. Then listen and check your answers.

1. Do you want to get ice cream or something to eat?
2. Does your apartment building have a laundry room?
3. Did you look upstairs in the bedrooms?
4. I did. But I can't find my cell phone anywhere.
5. Yeah, there's one downstairs, near the entryway.
6. Sure. There's a good coffee shop nearby.

C PAIRS Match the sentences in 3B to make three conversations.

Stress in compounds

A compound is a word made by putting two words together. We write some compounds as one word and some as two words. When the compound word is a noun, we usually stress the first part: li͏̇ving room. We also stress the first part in compounds with **any, every,** and **some**: e͏̇verything. When the compound word is an adverb of position, we usually stress the second part: outsi͏̇de.

---

4 LISTENING

A ▶09-19 Read the Listening Skill. Then listen to the first part of the story. What do you think the story is going to be about? Predict what you think will happen.

B ▶09-20 Listen to the entire story. Were your predictions correct?

C ▶09-20 Listen again. Circle the correct answers.
1. The man and his wife *moved to a new house / got a new cat / bought new furniture*.
2. They were *worried / angry / excited* about the change.
3. They looked for Tiger *in the attic / downstairs / in the basement* first.
4. They also searched the *closets and bedrooms / bedrooms and attic / attic and roof*.
5. The cat was probably *in the attic / in the moving van / outside* before he returned to the kitchen.

D PAIRS What do you think Tiger was doing when he disappeared?

LISTENING SKILL Predicting

When you're listening to a story or narration, you can understand it better if you make predictions about what you're going to hear or about the things that you think will happen. To practice the skill, listen to a short part of a passage, then stop to list the vocabulary, actions, or emotions that you hear. Then listen to the entire passage and check your predictions.

---

5 TRY IT YOURSELF

A MAKE IT PERSONAL Think about a time when you lost something. What happened? Where did you look for it? Where did you find it? Take notes.

B PAIRS Discuss your notes from 5A. Ask questions to get more information.
A: When I was visiting my grandparents, I lost a ring my boyfriend gave me.
B: Oh, wow. What happened?
A: I looked for it everywhere—in the bedroom…

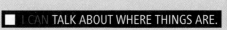
☐ I CAN TALK ABOUT WHERE THINGS ARE.

LESSON 4   READ PRODUCT REVIEWS

ALBA PARDO
@AlbaP

I just used this app to buy a new kitchen table. It was a great deal!

1 BEFORE YOU READ

A PAIRS Have you ever used an app to buy something for your home? How did it work? If not, what kind of app do you think could be useful?

I used an app to buy...

B VOCABULARY ▶09-21 Listen. Then listen and repeat.

> **goods:** things which are made and sold
>
> **used:** something that is not new and has already had an owner
>
> **directly:** with no other person or thing involved
>
> **a dropdown menu:** a list of choices that appears on a screen when you click on a menu
>
> **browse:** to look for information on the Internet or on a website
>
> **a search engine:** a computer program that helps you find information on the Internet

>> FOR PRACTICE, GO TO PAGE 157

2 READ

A PREVIEW Look at the title and scan the reviews. What do you think they are about?

B ▶09-22 Listen. Read the online reviews.

Howl Reviews

Used NeighborGoods to get my furniture

Marina V. Has anyone used the NeighborGoods App to buy used stuff? If so, what did you think of it? I'd love to know how it works.

Carlos B. Marina, I use NeighborGoods all the time—it's great. When I first heard about it, I had never used an app to buy things directly from people. But I did a search and the online reviews were positive, so I decided to check it out.

You're going to like how easy it is to use. First, you choose your city from a
5 list in a dropdown menu. Then you can look for items by browsing through categories or by typing in exactly what you want in the site's search engine. The app connects you to items that people are giving away or selling within five miles of your address. Now, I know what you're thinking: How can you trust someone you've never met? Well, the app checks everyone's personal
10 information when they join, so I think it's safe to use.

Here's what I like about it. It's great if you're looking for interesting or inexpensive furniture, clothes, or even children's toys. There are a lot of great items. And because it only searches locally, you don't have to waste time or money traveling too far away.

15 Dan M. I love this app! I used it to find furniture for my apartment. I recently moved, and I needed a lot of things—everything really. Plus, I didn't have much money.

I browsed through the furniture section, and there was a lot to choose from. I realized that a lot of the furniture I liked was from one seller. It was a couple
20 who lived right around the corner. I bought a bed, two end tables, and a bookcase, and it only cost me $100. It was such a great deal!

NeighborGoods is a smart way to find lots of inexpensive stuff. But my favorite thing about using the app was getting to meet my neighbors! The couple that I met was really nice and friendly. They told me everything I needed to know
25 about the neighborhood. You should definitely give NeighborGoods a try!

108   UNIT 9

3 CHECK YOUR UNDERSTANDING

A Which statement best describes the main idea of the reviews?

a. NeighborGoods is the best way to learn about your neighborhood.

b. NeighborGoods is a good way to find used items.

c. NeighborGoods is the best app available.

B Read the reviews again. Circle the correct answers. There is more than one correct answer.

1. Why does Carlos like NeighborGoods?

   a. It helps him make friends.

   b. It is a good way to find interesting stuff.

   c. It helps him find things nearby.

   d. It is safe to use.

2. How did Carlos find and learn about the app?

   a. A good friend told him about it.

   b. He found it through a search engine.

   c. He read online reviews about it.

   d. He saw an online ad.

3. Why did Dan decide to use the app?

   a. He needed furniture.

   b. He had just moved to the area.

   c. He needed children's toys.

   d. He wanted to make new friends.

4. What do they both like about the app?

   a. It has inexpensive stuff.

   b. It's a great way to meet people.

   c. It has a lot of items to choose from.

   d. It only has really nice stuff.

C FOCUS ON LANGUAGE Reread lines 3-8 in the reviews. Think about the phrases *check it out* and *within five miles*. Circle the correct answers.

1. When Carlos *checked out* the website, he ___ .

   a. paid to be able to use it

   b. researched it to learn more about it

   c. paid for items online

2. The phrase *within five miles* means ___ .

   a. five miles or less   b. more than five miles   c. exactly five miles

> **READING SKILL Identify fact vs. opinion**
>
> When you are reading something, it is important to notice the difference between facts and opinions. A fact is a piece of information that is true. An opinion is someone's preference or idea. An opinion will vary from person to person.

D Read the Reading Skill. Read the statements and write *fact* or *opinion*.

_____ 1. NeighborGoods finds you items within five miles of your address.

_____ 2. $100 for a bed, two end tables, and a bookcase is a great deal!

_____ 3. NeighborGoods has positive online reviews.

_____ 4. NeighborGoods is a smart way to find inexpensive stuff.

_____ 5. The best thing about NeighborGoods is meeting new people.

E PAIRS What are the reviews about? Retell the most important ideas. Use your own words.

The reviews talk about an online app and how...

> Find out about other similar apps and how they work. 🔍

4 MAKE IT PERSONAL

A Think about the reviews. What are some of your favorite apps? Complete the chart.

App	What does it do?	Why do you like it?

B PAIRS Tell your partner about your favorite app. Discuss.

My favorite app is...

☐ I CAN READ PRODUCT REVIEWS.

ALBA PARDO
@AlbaP

I just wrote a blog post about the home of my dreams. Now I just need some money to build it. 😊

1 BEFORE YOU WRITE

A What is the nicest home you've ever seen? What did it look like?

B Alba wrote a blog post about her dream home. Where does she want to build it?

Blog | About | Destinations | Contact 🔍 Search

My Dream Home

I'm going to build my dream home in the mountains in Costa Rica. I love the beautiful views and the amazing plants and animals in these mountains.

The house will have a long, wide porch across the front, lots of windows, and a big garden. I will sit on the porch every evening in a comfortable chair and watch the sun set.

The living room will be at the front of the house. It will have tall windows so the morning sun can come in. The kitchen and laundry room will be at the back of the house. There will be a door from the kitchen out to a stone patio with an extra dining area. The upstairs will have three bedrooms, each with a big closet. There will be a garden in the backyard. I'm going to grow fresh vegetables and fruits. I will also raise goats so we can have fresh goat's milk and make cheese.

I'm going to invite all my friends and family to visit. I hope my dream comes true someday!

About
RSS Feed
Social Media
Recent Posts
Archives
Email

Leave a reply

Enter your comment here…

C Read the blog post again. What kinds of details does Alba include about her home? Complete the chart.

Locations	Places	Details
Location of home	in the mountains in Costa Rica	beautiful views, amazing plants and animals
Outside areas	porch	
Inside rooms		

2 FOCUS ON WRITING

A Read the Writing Skill.

B Look at three incorrect sentences from Alba's first draft of her blog post. Underline the parts that are not parallel.

1. The house will have a long, wide porch across the front, lots of windows, and a big gardening.
2. I will sit on the porch every evening in a comfortable chair and watching the sun set.
3. I will also raise goats so we can have fresh goat's milk and making cheese.

C Look at the sentences in 2B again. Underline the corrected parts of the sentences in the model in 1B.

> **WRITING SKILL Use parallel structure**
>
> Use the same pattern of words to show that two or more ideas have the same level of importance. These ideas can be words, phrases, or clauses. They are usually joined by conjunctions, such as *and* or *or*.
>
> Incorrect: *Wei passed the class because he studied for exams, turned in all his homework, and his love of the subject.*
>
> Correct: *Wei passed the class because he studied for exams, turned in all his homework, and loved the subject.*

3 PLAN YOUR WRITING

A Think about your dream home. What would it look like? Complete the chart.

Locations	Places	Details
Location of home		
Outside areas		
Inside rooms		

B PAIRS Discuss your ideas.

My dream home will have...

4 WRITE

Write a blog post about the dream home you described in 3A. Remember to make all the phrases and clauses in your sentences parallel. Use the post in 1B as a model.

5 REVISE YOUR WRITING

A PAIRS Exchange posts and read your partner's.
1. Did your partner describe his or her dream home and provide details about it?
2. Did your partner make the words, phrases, and clauses parallel?

B PAIRS Can your partner improve his or her post? Make suggestions.

> Check your
> • spelling
> • punctuation
> • capitalization

6 PROOFREAD

Read your post again. Can you improve your writing?

■ I CAN WRITE ABOUT MY DREAM HOME.

PUT IT TOGETHER

1 MEDIA PROJECT

 A ▶09-23 Listen or watch. What does Boris want to do?

 B ▶09-23 Listen or watch again. Answer the questions.

1. What furniture is Boris going to buy? _____
2. Where is he going to put the furniture? _____
3. Why does he want to buy each piece of furniture?

_____

C Make your own video.

Step 1 Think about a room or area of your home that you would like to redecorate. Think about what furniture you will need to buy.

Step 2 Make a 30-second video. Show the room or area in your home. Say what furniture you need, where you will put it, and why you want it.

Step 3 Share your video. Answer questions and get feedback.

2 LEARNING STRATEGY

> **PRACTICE WORD STRESS FOR PRONUNCIATION**
>
> When you study new vocabulary, put a dot over the stressed syllable. You can do this in your book or on flashcards. Use a dictionary to help you. For example, a dictionary shows the stress for *bookcase* like this /ˈbʊk-keɪs/. The symbol ' at the beginning of the word shows that the first syllable is stressed. So, in this example, you would put a dot over the first syllable of *bookcase*.

bȯokcase: noun, a piece of furniture with shelves to hold books

Find words in the unit that are difficult to pronounce. Put a dot over the stressed syllable. Use a dictionary to help you. Then practice saying the words aloud. Pay attention to the word stress.

3 REFLECT AND PLAN

A Look back through the unit. Check (✓) the things you learned. Highlight the things you need to learn.

Speaking objectives
- [ ] Talk about plans
- [ ] Talk about reasons for being late
- [ ] Talk about where things are

Vocabulary
- [ ] Living room furniture and decor
- [ ] Reasons for being late
- [ ] Places in and around the house

Pronunciation
- [ ] The letter *a*
- [ ] Stress in compounds

Grammar
- [ ] Future with *will*, *be going to*, present continuous, and simple present
- [ ] Indirect questions
- [ ] Adverbs and adverbial phrases of place

Reading
- [ ] Identify fact vs. opinion

Writing
- [ ] Use parallel structure

B What will you do to learn the things you highlighted? For example, use your app, review your Student Book, or do other practice. Make a plan.

Notes   Done

In the app, watch the Grammar Coach video: Adverbs and adverbial phrases of place

_____
_____
_____
_____

10 HOW LONG DID YOU WORK THERE?

LEARNING GOALS

In this unit, you
⊗ start a job interview
⊗ talk about your work experience
⊗ give more details about your work experience
⊗ read interview advice
⊗ write a cover letter

GET STARTED

A Read the unit title and learning goals.

B Look at the photo of an interview. What do you see?

C Now read Mandy's message. What is she interviewing people for?

MANDY WILSON
@MandyW

Interviewing people for the open marketing position this week. Hope to hire someone soon!

MANDY WILSON
@MandyW

I'm always nervous at job interviews—even when I'm the interviewer!

 1 VOCABULARY Job interviews

A ▶10-01 **Listen. Then listen and repeat.**

a position: a job, or a title
a candidate: someone who is being considered for a job
human resources (HR): the department in a company that deals with hiring, training, and helping employees
an application: a formal, written request for a job, usually a form

a résumé: a written description of your education, abilities, and jobs
a cover letter: a letter you write that goes with your résumé, highlighting details about your work experience
a reference: someone who knows you well and can write a letter about you
a skill: an ability to do something well

B **Complete the conversations with words from 1A.**

1. A: I'm applying for a job at TSW Media.
   B: That's great. Feel free to use me as a _____ .

2. A: My brother filled out an _____ for a job.
   B: What _____ did he apply for?

3. A: Did you interview a lot of people?
   B: Yes, but there was only one good _____ .

4. A: Who should I send my _____ to?
   B: I'm not sure. You should call _____ .

C PAIRS **Have you ever applied for a job? Discuss the steps you took.**

2 GRAMMAR Tag questions

A tag question is a question added to the end of a sentence. Use an auxiliary verb and the subject of the sentence in a tag question. Speakers sometimes use tag questions to confirm information. When the main verb of the sentence is affirmative, the tag question is negative.

Affirmative sentence	Negative tag
She's here for the interview,	**isn't she**?
I've given you a copy of my résumé,	**haven't I**?
They'll be here soon,	**won't they**?

I am becomes *aren't I* in a negative tag. *I'm a little late today,* **aren't I**?

When the main verb of the sentence is negative, the tag question is affirmative.

Negative sentence	Affirmative tag
You didn't have any trouble,	**did you**?
The interviews haven't started yet,	**have they**?
We can't park here,	**can we**?

Notes
- When the questioner's statement is correct, we use *yes* to agree with an affirmative sentence and *no* to agree with a negative sentence. The verb in the answer agrees with the main verb in the sentence.
- When the questioner's statement is **not** correct, we use *no* to disagree with an affirmative sentence and *yes* to disagree with a negative sentence. The verb in the answer contradicts the main verb in the sentence.

>> FOR PRACTICE, GO TO PAGE 152

3 PRONUNCIATION

A ▶10-03 Listen. Notice the stressed syllable in each word. Then listen and repeat.

ref•e•rence   ré•su•mé   de•part•ment   ap•pli•ca•tion

B ▶10-04 Circle the word that does *not* have the stress shown. Then listen and check your answers.

1. ••   office   apply   business   cover
2. •••   position   directions   designer   manager
3. •••   company   computer   candidate   interview
4. ••••   information   education   experience   conversation

C PAIRS Write one more word for each line in 3B with the stress shown.

> **Stressed syllables in nouns**
>
> It can be hard to predict the stressed syllable in a word, but there are some rules that can help. In most nouns with two syllables, we stress the first syllable: let•ter. In most nouns with three syllables, we stress the first or second syllable: ré•su•mé, de•part•ment. In nouns that end in -*tion*, we stress the syllable just before -*tion*: ap•pli•ca•tion.

4 CONVERSATION

A ▶10-05 Listen or watch. Circle the correct answers.

1. When Mandy first sees Joanne, she ___.
   a. takes her coat   b. shakes her hand   c. offers her a drink
2. Joanne is in the office for ___.
   a. a job interview   b. a market research conference   c. a lunch meeting
3. Joanne meets with human resources to ___.
   a. give them her information   b. fill out paperwork   c. ask questions
4. Mandy asks Joanne to ___.
   a. put on her coat   b. get her coffee   c. have a seat

B ▶10-06 Listen or watch. Complete the conversation.

Mandy: Thanks for coming in for the interview today.

Joanne: I'm happy to be here.

Mandy: You _____ have any trouble finding the office, _____ ?

Joanne: No, not at all. Thank you.

Mandy: Great. I have a copy of your résumé and cover letter. Let's get started.

C ▶10-07 Listen and repeat. Then practice with a partner.

5 TRY IT YOURSELF

A WALK AROUND Start job interviews and talk to as many classmates as you can. Write down the names of all the people you talk to, and the jobs they're interested in.

A: You're here to interview for the assistant designer position, aren't you?
B: Yes, I am. I'm Marta Rivas.
A: It's nice to meet you, Marta. I'm Chris Kim. I will be interviewing you today.

B CLASS Report to the class. How many classmates did you interview? What jobs were they interested in?

☐ I CAN START A JOB INTERVIEW.

MANDY WILSON
@MandyW

I learn so much by listening to people at job interviews!

 1 VOCABULARY Work experience

A ▶10-08 Listen. Then listen and repeat.

manage a team

train new employees

create a budget

give a presentation

write a report

communicate with team members

resolve a problem

meet a deadline

B ▶10-09 Listen to the descriptions. Number the pictures in 1A.

C PAIRS Look at the tasks in 1A. Brainstorm 3-5 jobs that need these skills.

Managers need to create budgets.

2 GRAMMAR Present perfect with *for* and *since; how long* and *ever*

Use the present perfect with *for* and *since* to talk about something that began in the past and continues up to now.

Present perfect statements with *for* and *since*					
Subject	*Have / Has*	*Not*	Past participle		*For / Since*
I / We / They	have		worked	there	**for** six months.
He / She	has	not	been		**since** 2017.

To ask about something that began in the past and continues up to now, use *how long*.

Question with *how long*					Short answers
How long	*Have*	Subject	Past participle		
How long	have	you	worked	there?	**For** a few weeks. / **Since** last month.

To ask about something that happened at a non-specific time in the past, use *ever*.

Question with *ever*					Short answers	
Have	Subject	*Ever*	Past participle		Affirmative	Negative
Have	you	ever	managed	a team?	Yes, I **have**.	No, I **haven't**.

Notes
- Use *for* + a length of time to show how long something lasted.
- Use *since* + a point in time to show when something started.
- Use the simple past, not the present perfect, to refer to events that happened at a specific time in the past. *He **has given** a presentation on this topic.* = exact time is not clear
  *He **gave** a presentation on this topic **in March**.* = *in March* is a specific time in the past

>> FOR PRACTICE, GO TO PAGE 153

3 PRONUNCIATION

A ▶10-11 Listen. Notice the weak and contracted pronunciations of *have* and *has*. Then listen and repeat.

A: How long *have* you been a manager?
B: I've been a manager for six months.
A: How long *has* she worked there?
B: She's worked there for two years.

> **Weak and contracted pronunciations of *have* and *has***
>
> *Have* and *has* usually have a weak or contracted pronunciation when they come before another word. When *have* and *has* come *after* another word, the *h* is often silent. Notice that the contracted form of *has* sounds the same as the contracted form of *is*.

B ▶10-12 Listen. Circle the word you hear. Then listen and repeat.

1. I / I've had a lot of different jobs.
2. I / I've studied computer science.
3. I / I've worked in a restaurant for two years.
4. I / I've managed a business.
5. I / I've lived in another country.
6. I / I've trained other employees.

C PAIRS Talk about the statements in 3B. Which statements are true for you?

4 CONVERSATION

A ▶10-13 Listen or watch. Circle the correct answers.

1. Joanne started as a marketing *manager* / *analyst* / *assistant*.
2. She has managed two small teams since she
   started her career / *became an analyst* / *became a team leader*.
3. Problem-solving is a *big* / *fun* / *small* part of her job.
4. She feels proudest about *her first project* /
   being a team leader / *meeting her deadlines*.

B ▶10-14 Listen or watch. Complete the conversation.

Mandy: How long _____ at your current job?
Joanne: I've worked there for five years.
Mandy: OK. Have you ever managed a team?
Joanne: Yes, I've managed two small teams _____ I started.
Mandy: That's great. What's the hardest part of being a team leader?
Joanne: For me, it's having to solve all of the problems that come up.

C ▶10-15 Listen and repeat. Then practice with a partner.

D PAIRS Make new conversations. Use the words in 1A or your own ideas.

5 TRY IT YOURSELF

A MAKE IT PERSONAL Look at the list of jobs and skills in 1C. Choose one job from the list.

B ROLE PLAY Student A, you are a candidate applying for this job. Student B, you are the interviewer. Ask about his or her experience.

A: Have you ever given a presentation?
B: Yes, I've given many presentations since I was hired.

GIVE MORE DETAILS ABOUT YOUR WORK EXPERIENCE

MANDY WILSON

@MandyW

The average interview is 40 minutes long but 33% of managers know within the first 90 seconds if they're going to hire that candidate.

 1 VOCABULARY Soft skills

A ▶10-16 Listen. Then listen and repeat.

> **give feedback:** to tell someone how well they have or haven't done something, and usually how they can improve
> **manage your time:** to use your time in a productive and useful way
> **stay focused:** to pay attention to a specific thing
> **think outside the box:** to think creatively using original ideas
> **show leadership:** to take actions that show you are good at leading people
> **work as a team:** to work with a group of people, as on a project
> **work independently:** to do your job by yourself, without supervision
> **think critically:** to use logic to think carefully about something
> **deal with conflict:** to help solve problems between people
> **handle challenges:** to manage problems or tasks that are difficult or complicated
> **build good relationships:** to develop positive connections with other people

B Put the soft skills from 1A in the correct category.

Things you do alone — Both — Things you do with other people

C PAIRS Compare your answers in 1B. Add another soft skill to each category.

 2 GRAMMAR Information questions with the present perfect

COACH

To ask information questions with the present perfect, use a question word + *have / has* + the past participle.

Question word	*Have / Has*	Subject	Past participle	
What		you	**tried**	to change?
Why	have	we	**waited**	so long?
Where		they	**worked**	in the past?
Who		he	**worked**	with on a team?
How	has	she	**dealt**	with conflict?
When		he	**shown**	leadership?

Notes
- It's possible to use *what* + a noun. **What problems** *have you solved?*
- It's possible to use *how* + *much / many* + a noun.
  How much time *have we spent on this project?*   **How many interviews** *have you had?*

>> FOR PRACTICE, GO TO PAGE 154

3 CONVERSATION

 A ▶10-18 **Listen or watch. Circle the correct answers.**

1. What does Joanne say is one of her strengths?
   a. She is very positive.
   b. She is very friendly.
   c. She is very creative.
2. Why does Joanne think feedback is important?
   a. It helps her understand how to improve.
   b. It helps her think critically.
   c. It helps her resolve problems.
3. What difficult situation did Joanne have at work?
   a. She wasn't giving good feedback to her team members.
   b. She had some team members who weren't getting along.
   c. She didn't know how to build good relationships.
4. What did she do to resolve this conflict?
   a. She helped them to see each other's point of view.
   b. She met with them as a group to discuss the issue.
   c. She divided up the team.

> **CONVERSATION SKILL**
> **Express an opinion**
>
> To express an opinion, say: *In my opinion…, It seems to me (that)…, I feel that…, In my experience…, I believe (that)…, I think (that)…,* or *I find (that)…*
>
> **A:** Tell me about your strengths, Joanne.
> **B:** I believe that I deal with challenges well.
>
> Listen to or watch the conversation in 3A again. Underline the expressions that you hear above.

 B ▶10-19 **Listen or watch. Complete the conversation.**

Mandy: What are your strengths?

Joanne: I welcome feedback and I use it to make my work better. I think that's very important.

Mandy: Can you give me an example? _____ you used feedback?

Joanne: Sure. I share my ideas with my colleagues and I ask for feedback. I use their ideas to improve my work.

Mandy: That's interesting. Are there any work skills you're still working on? _____ you done specifically?

Joanne: I've worked hard to manage my time better. I've learned that it's OK to sometimes let things go.

C ▶10-20 **Listen and repeat. Then practice with a partner.**

D PAIRS **Make new conversations. Use the words in 1A or your own ideas.**

4 TRY IT YOURSELF

A MAKE IT PERSONAL **What soft skills do you have? What are your strengths? Take notes.**

B PAIRS **Tell a partner about your soft skills and strengths. Ask questions to get more information.**

A: In my opinion, I manage my time well.
B: When have you used this skill?

MANDY WILSON
@MandyW

Great article with some helpful interview tips. A good read for anyone who's preparing for an interview.

1 BEFORE YOU READ

A PAIRS Have you ever had an interview to get a job or to get into a school? What happened? Talk about it.

I went on an interview for...

B VOCABULARY ▶10-21 Listen. Then listen and repeat.

> **a positive attitude**: to think or feel in a happy or hopeful way about someone or something
> **a tip**: advice or something you say to help someone
> **impressive**: very good or great
> **mumble**: to speak very quietly and not clearly
> **convince**: to make someone think or believe something
> **body language**: showing thoughts and feelings through movements rather than spoken words
> **slouch**: to stand, sit, or walk with your shoulders bent forward
> **fidget**: to keep moving your hands or feet because you are bored or nervous

>> FOR PRACTICE, GO TO PAGE 158

2 READ

A PREVIEW Look at the title. What do you think the article is about?

B ▶10-22 Listen. Read the article.

INTERVIEWS: MORE THAN JUST THE BASICS!

Everyone knows (or should know) the basics about going on a job interview. You need to be on time. You should have a positive attitude and dress well. You also need to know about the company and the position. These are all helpful tips, aren't they? But sometimes, even if someone gets all those things right, the interview can still go very, very wrong. I should know—I've worked in
5 human resources for 20 years! Here are the most common mistakes I've seen in an interview.

It is important to look relaxed and confident in an interview.

Right Candidate, Poor Interview Skills

The perfect candidate applied for a position in our sales department. His application and résumé were impressive, but he was really
10 shy and nervous. He wouldn't even make eye contact. Throughout the interview, he mumbled his answers to all my questions and spoke really quickly. His interview skills convinced me that he wasn't a good fit for this position.

15 When you're at an interview, it's important to make good eye contact, but look away once in a while so you don't make the interviewer uncomfortable. If you feel nervous, pause to think about your answers before you speak.
20 It's also okay to speak slowly. Speaking slowly is better than speaking too quickly.

Incorrect Body Language

A candidate came in to interview for a project manager position and she made a great first impression. She had all
25 the right answers to my questions. Sounds great, doesn't it? Well, during the interview she kept looking at her watch. She couldn't sit still, and she kept crossing her arms. Her body language was telling me that she didn't want to be in the interview.

30 During an interview, pay attention to what your body is doing. Your body movements are just as important as your answers to the questions—they're a language of their own. First, remember the basics: Sit up straight and don't slouch in your chair. Then remember to be still when you're
35 listening and to think about each movement when you're talking. And of course, avoid nervous habits like crossing your arms, shaking your legs, or fidgeting in general.

3 CHECK YOUR UNDERSTANDING

A Which statement best describes the main idea of the article?

    a. The way you speak is more important than the way you move in interviews.

    b. Most people make mistakes in interviews and don't get the job.

    c. How you speak and move are both important during interviews.

B Read the article again. Circle the correct answers.

    1. Why did the first person described in the article not get the job?

        a. He spoke too slowly and seemed uninterested.

        b. He mumbled and didn't look at the interviewer.

        c. He was not prepared for the interview.

    2. What did the interviewer not like about the second person described in the article?

        a. She didn't seem interested in the position.

        b. She didn't have good answers to the questions.

        c. She didn't know anything about the company.

    3. Why did the author choose these interview examples for the article?

        a. They show the most common interview mistakes people make.

        b. They show that most people are bad at doing job interviews.

        c. They show the worst interview mistakes she has ever seen.

    4. Why is the author a good source of information about interviewing?

        a. She has a lot of experience looking for work.

        b. She only ever worked for one company.

        c. She has been interviewing people for many years.

C FOCUS ON LANGUAGE Reread lines 13–24 in the article. Think about the phrases *a good fit* and *a first impression*. Then answer the questions.

> **READING SKILL** Make associations
>
> When you read, think about what you already know about the subject of the text. Think about other texts you have read and experiences you have had that can help you understand what you are reading.

    1. What does the author mean by the phrase *a good fit*?

        _____

    2. What does *a first impression* mean?

        _____

D Read the Reading Skill. Answer the questions.

    1. What else have you read about interviews? What kind of advice does the article give that is similar or different?

        _____

    2. What experience have you had with interviews? How does this experience help you understand the examples in the article?

        _____

E PAIRS What is the article about? Retell the most important ideas. Use your own words.

The article is about job interviews and...

> Find out about other interviewing tips. 🔍

4 MAKE IT PERSONAL

A Think about the article you just read. Brainstorm. What other things or behaviors are important during an interview? How or why are they important?

B CLASS Take a survey. Make a list of all the things and behaviors from 4A.

■ I CAN READ INTERVIEW ADVICE.

LESSON 5   WRITE A COVER LETTER

MANDY WILSON
@MandyW

I've seen a lot of great résumés. But I'm surprised that people don't spend more time on their cover letters!

1 BEFORE YOU WRITE

A Have you ever written or read a cover letter? What do you think needs to be included?

B Joanne sent this cover letter with her résumé. What position is she applying for?

> Joanne Martin
> 40 Grove Street
> New York, NY 10001
>
> Mandy Wilson
> Market Researcher, TSW Media
> 100 Main Street
> New York, NY 10001
>
> September 17, 2019
>
> Dear Ms. Wilson:
>
> I am writing in response to the open marketing position with TSW Media. I believe I am a strong candidate for the position.
>
> I have worked at Parrot Creative for five years. During that time, I have gained the experience needed to face the challenges of this position. For example, I led the marketing team that was responsible for creating a new line of products. I also developed new market research surveys for many different clients. Finally, I improved the company's overall sales by leading creative marketing campaigns.
>
> I love working as part of a team and enjoy building strong relationships with my colleagues. I am comfortable with both giving and receiving feedback. I can think outside of the box when my team is brainstorming ideas, but when it is time to build a plan, I stay focused to meet the deadline.
>
> I have attached my résumé, which has more information about my skills, work experience, and education. I look forward to hearing from you. Thank you for considering my application.
>
> Sincerely,
>
> Joanne Martin

C Read the letter again. Notice how it is organized. What kinds of details does Joanne include?

Purpose	Details
Start the letter *contact information, date, and greeting*	includes names, addresses, the date, and a greeting
Paragraph 1 *why she is writing*	
Paragraph 2 *past experience that relates to the job*	
Paragraph 3 *skills that relate to the job*	
End the letter *thank you and closing*	

2 FOCUS ON WRITING

A Read the Writing Skill.

B Read the letter again. Answer the questions.

1. Who is the audience?

_____

2. What does the audience need and want to know?

_____

_____

3. What language, style, and tone does Joanne use?

_____

_____

3 PLAN YOUR WRITING

A Imagine you are responding to a posting for a job that you're interested in. Complete the chart.

Purpose	Details
Start the letter *contact information, date, and greeting*	
Paragraph 1 *why you are writing*	
Paragraph 2 *past experience that relates to the job*	
Paragraph 3 *skills that relate to the job*	
End the letter *thank you and closing*	

B PAIRS Discuss your ideas. *In the first paragraph, I will include...*

4 WRITE

Write a cover letter using the information from 3A. Remember your audience. Use the letter in 1B as a model.

5 REVISE YOUR WRITING

A PAIRS Exchange letters and read your partner's.

1. Did your partner explain why he or she is writing?
2. Did your partner include important past experience and skills that relate to the job?
3. Did your partner remember the audience?

B PAIRS Can your partner improve his or her letter? Make suggestions.

Check your
• spelling
• punctuation
• capitalization

6 PROOFREAD

Read your letter again. Can you improve your writing?

☐ I CAN WRITE A COVER LETTER.

PUT IT TOGETHER

1 MEDIA PROJECT

▶ **A** ▶10-23 Listen or watch. What does Alex talk about?

▶ **B** ▶10-23 Listen or watch again. Answer the questions.

1. What is Alex's dream job? _____
2. What skills or experience does he already have? _____
   _____
3. What skills or experience does he still need? _____
   _____

C Make your own video.

Step 1 Think of your dream job or a job you're interested in. What skills and experience do you already have? What skills and experience do you still need?

Step 2 Make a 30-second video. Talk about the skills you already have, and the skills that you still need.

Step 3 Share your video. Answer questions and get feedback.

2 LEARNING STRATEGY

┌───┐
│ **TELL A STORY TO PRACTICE VERB TENSES**   │
│ Telling a story about an event, or moment, can help │
│ you practice verb tenses. Choose a moment to talk │
│ about in the past, present, or future. Then choose │
│ the correct verb tense to talk about that moment. │
└───┘

I've been a cook in Italian and Chinese restaurants. I've also worked as a restaurant manager.

Practice the present perfect tense by writing about a past event without saying a specific time. Practice by reading your stories aloud.

3 REFLECT AND PLAN

A Look back through the unit. Check (✓) the things you learned. Highlight the things you need to learn.

Speaking objectives
- ☐ Start a job interview
- ☐ Talk about your work experience
- ☐ Give more details about your work experience

Vocabulary
- ☐ Job interviews
- ☐ Work experience
- ☐ Soft skills

Pronunciation
- ☐ Stressed syllables in nouns
- ☐ Weak and contracted pronunciations of *have* and *has*

Grammar
- ☐ Tag questions
- ☐ Present perfect with *for* and *since*; *how long* and *ever*
- ☐ Information questions with the present perfect

Reading
- ☐ Make associations

Writing
- ☐ Consider your audience

B What will you do to learn the things you highlighted? For example, use your app, review your Student Book, or do other practice. Make a plan.

Review the Writing Skill: Consider your audience, page 123.

A ▶01-02 Listen to the conversations. Is the action happening now, in the future, or is this a temporary situation? Check (✓) the correct box.

	1	2	3	4	5	6	7	8
now / at the moment								
future	✓							
temporary situation								

B Complete the sentences with the present continuous form of the verbs in parentheses. Use contractions when possible.

I'm really enjoying my job this summer. I ___'m working___ with my friend Vanessa at
            1 (work)
a restaurant on weekends. The restaurant is going out of business at the end of the

summer, so we _____ for new jobs already. We _____ for jobs at
          2 (look)   **3 (not / look)**
another restaurant though. We're thinking about jobs that are related to our studies.

I _____ French so I'd love a job at the university. Vanessa _____ a degree
   4 (study)   **5 (get)**
in business. She _____ for jobs at an office. Outside of work, I _____ a lot
       6 (apply)   **7 (play)**
of tennis and spending time with friends. Vanessa and her husband, Ben, _____
                                                    8 (move)
to a new apartment this month. They are very busy these days. They want to go on vacation,

but they _____ anytime soon.
     9 (not / travel)

C Complete the conversations with the verbs in parentheses. Use the present continuous for temporary situations. Use the simple present if the situation is *not* temporary. Use contractions when possible.

1. A: _____Do you live_____ here in New York?
           (you / live)
   B: No, I don't. I 'm visiting _____ my family.
                  (visit)

2. A: How long _____ here?
             (Ana / stay)
   B: She _____ a few weeks with her sisters.
            (spend)

3. A: What _____ these days?
           (your parents / do)
   B: They're on vacation. They _____ by train around Europe.
                  (travel)

4. A: _____ any classes this spring?
        (you / take)
   B: Yes, I _____ Japanese.
         (study)

5. A: Where _____ ?
        (you / work)
   B: I _____ a job at the hospital. I really like it.
        (have)

6. A: Your brother is a good tennis player. _____ on a team?
                                (he / play)
   B: Yes, he does. He _____ on his college team.
           (be)

7. A: _____ for a job?
      (your brother / still / look)
   B: No, he's very busy with school. He _____ right now.
                       (not / work)

A ▶01-09 Listen to the sentences. Check (✓) the sentence that happened first.

1. ☐ David was upset.
   ✓ He heard the news.
2. ☐ Oscar looked for a new job.
   ☐ He got married.
3. ☐ Kevin took some classes.
   ☐ He found a new job.
4. ☐ Dina applied to graduate school.
   ☐ She graduated from college.

5. ☐ Miriam started her own business.
   ☐ She got engaged.
6. ☐ Nora adopted a pet.
   ☐ She moved to a larger apartment.
7. ☐ Jim and Ann moved to a new house.
   ☐ They had a baby.
8. ☐ Mark changed careers.
   ☐ He got a certificate in teaching.

B The timeline shows important events in Mike's life. Complete the sentences with *before, after,* or *when*. More than one answer may be possible.

2012	2013	2014	2015	2016	2017
studied English	traveled to Europe worked in a restaurant	graduated from college	took piano lessons	got engaged moved to Boston	applied to graduate school

1. Mike studied English ____before____ he graduated from college.
2. _____ Mike graduated from college, he traveled to Europe.
3. Mike took piano lessons _____ he graduated from college.
4. _____ Mike traveled to Europe, he worked in a restaurant.
5. Mike traveled to Europe _____ he took piano lessons.
6. Mike graduated from college _____ he got engaged.
7. Mike moved to Boston _____ he got engaged.
8. _____ Mike moved to Boston, he applied to graduate school.

C Combine the sentences into one sentence. Add commas when necessary.

1. First: I graduated from college.
   Then: I got engaged.
   ____I got engaged____ after
   ____I graduated from college____ .

2. First: Hiro lost his job.
   Then: Hiro changed careers.
   _____ when
   _____ .

3. First: Jane went to the conference.
   Then: Jane met some old friends.
   _____ when
   _____ .

4. First: Jackie didn't finish her homework.
   Then: Jackie ate dinner.
   _____ before
   _____ .

5. First: We took an online course.
   Then: We learned a lot about computers.
   When _____
   _____ .

6. First: The president walked into the room.
   Then: Everyone stood up.
   When _____
   _____ .

7. First: The office moved to another city.
   Then: Many employees quit.
   After _____
   _____ .

8. First: Lee didn't study English.
   Then: Lee moved to San Francisco.
   Before _____
   _____ .

A ▶01-16 Listen. Complete the conversation with the words you hear.

A: What do you want to do tonight?

B: _____Why don't we_____ go to a concert?
   ₁

A: _____ go to a concert. They're so loud! I want to do
   ₂
something quiet.

B: OK. _____ go on a walking tour of the city?
   ₃

A: No, it's too cold. _____ do something indoors.
   ₄

B: Hmm. Let me think. Do you like art? _____ go to a museum?
   ₅

A: I don't really like museums.

B: OK. I know! _____ go shopping.
   ₆

A: OK, sounds great. Do you want to have dinner first? _____
   ₇
go to a sushi place.

B: We always get sushi. _____ have sushi again.
   ₈

A: _____ try that new French restaurant?
   ₉

B: Perfect!

B Make suggestions with *why don't*, *let's*, or *let's not* and the words in parentheses. More than one answer may be possible.

1. A: What should we do for dinner tonight?

   B: _____Why don't we go to a restaurant?_____
      (go to a restaurant)

2. A: What do you want to do this weekend?

   B: _____
      (go to a concert)

3. A: Our meeting starts in an hour.

   B: _____
      (get some coffee first)

4. A: I'm really tired, and I'm not really interested in seeing the city.

   B: OK, _____
         (go sightseeing)

5. A: Jim and Kate are coming to town. What should they do?

   B: _____
      (go on a tour)

6. A: I need help with my Spanish homework.

   B: _____ She speaks Spanish.
      (ask Maya)

7. A: I need some postcards.

   B: OK, _____
         (go to a souvenir shop)

8. A: Do you want to go to the museum on Saturday?

   B: _____ . It's very busy on weekends. Weekdays are better.
      (go on Saturday)

9. A: I don't have a car. Can you give me a ride to the concert?

   B: Sure! _____
            (pick you up at 7:00)

A ▶02-02 Listen to the conversations. What is each item similar to? Match the answers. Write the letter on the line.

_c_ 1. chili   a. a party
___ 2. blanket   b. strawberries
___ 3. shampoo   c. chicken
___ 4. alarm clock   d. her sister
___ 5. Jenny   e. silk
___ 6. the noise   f. a fire alarm

B Complete the sentences with the correct form of *look, feel, smell, taste,* or *sound*. You will use some verbs more than once.

1. A: That's my parents when they were young.
   B: Nice picture. You _____look_____ a lot like your mom.

2. A: Do you hear that beeping noise?
   B: Yeah, it _____ like the microwave. I think Joe is making popcorn.

3. A: Are you baking something? It _____ like vanilla cake.
   B: No, that's actually a candle. Do you like it?

4. A: Have you tried one of these veggie burgers?
   B: Yes, but I didn't like it. It doesn't _____ like a real burger.

5. A: What's wrong? You look upset.
   B: It's this coffee. It smells good, but it _____ like dirt.

6. A: Your daughter _____ like a princess!
   B: Thanks! We're on our way to my sister's wedding. She's the flower girl.

7. A: Nice running shoes! Are they comfortable?
   B: No, they're not. They're heavy. They _____ like rocks.

C Complete the sentences. Use the words in parentheses with *like* to show similarity.

1. This soup _____tastes a lot like chicken_____ .
   (taste / a lot)

2. The office _____ .
   (smell / a lot)

3. Is that your report? It's so long! It _____ .
   (look)

4. This is an Asian pear. We eat them a lot in Korea. They _____ .
   (taste / a little)

5. Is that coffee? It _____ .
   (look)

6. Oh, no! What's on my coat? It's very sticky. It _____ .
   (feel)

7. We should leave the building. That _____ .
   (sound)

8. What kind of instrument is that? It _____ , but it's smaller.
   (look)

A ▶02-10 Listen to the conversation between a car salesman and a customer. Then check (✓) the sentences that are true.

1. ☐ Jim is ready to buy a car.
   ✓ Jim isn't ready to buy a car yet.
2. ☐ Jim is afraid to buy the wrong car.
   ☐ Mike is afraid to sell the wrong car.
3. ☐ Jim isn't happy to learn the price of the car.
   ☐ Jim isn't happy to see a sports car.

4. ☐ Jim is not ready to look at other cars.
   ☐ Jim is eager to look at sedans.
5. ☐ Mike is excited to show Jim a cheaper car.
   ☐ Mike is annoyed to show Jim more cars.
6. ☐ Jim is determined to do more research.
   ☐ Jim is determined to get a discount today.

B Complete the sentences with the correct form of *be* and the adjective and verb in parentheses. Use contractions when possible.

1. Daniel was very tired, but he ___was determined to finish___ the report before he went to bed.
   (determined / finish)
2. John works hard. He _____ an award from his company last year.
   (proud / get)
3. Camila has never been to China. She _____ there next month.
   (eager / travel)
4. Jonah needs to finish a report. He _____ home yet.
   (not ready / go)
5. I don't know how to use that computer software, but I _____ .
   (willing / learn)
6. Mark needs help, but he _____ .
   (ashamed / ask)
7. If you have questions, ask Kevin. He _____ .
   (happy / help)
8. Maya's handwriting _____ . I can't understand her note.
   (not easy / read)
9. My classmates speak English very well, but they _____ mistakes.
   (afraid / make)

C Read the situation. Write sentences with the words.

1. Chris got a job in another country. He's excited, but he doesn't know if he should take it.
   He / delighted / get / this exciting offer.
   _____He's delighted to get this exciting offer_____ .
   It / hard / move / far away from his friends.

   _____ .

2. Michael is always late for work. He lost his job at the bank.
   He / ashamed / tell / his friends.

   _____ .

   He / determined / find / a new job soon.

   _____ .

3. Clara is a terrible cook, but this cake recipe is very simple. Anyone can make it.
   This cake / not difficult / make.

   _____ .

   Clara / willing / try / this recipe.

   _____ .

4. No one in Justin's family has a college degree. Justin is graduating from college next month.
   Justin / eager / graduate / from college.

   _____ .

   His parents / proud / see / him graduate.

   _____ .

A ▶02-17 **Listen to the conversations. Then check (✓) the sentence that should come next.**

1. ☐ He is ready to go to work.
   ✓ He is ready to go home.
2. ☐ She needs swimming lessons.
   ☐ She doesn't need swimming lessons.
3. ☐ He makes a lot of mistakes.
   ☐ He doesn't make many mistakes.
4. ☐ There was a lot of traffic.
   ☐ There wasn't much traffic.
5. ☐ Her patients don't trust her.
   ☐ Her patients trust her.
6. ☐ He'll get a good grade.
   ☐ He'll get a bad grade.
7. ☐ No one could hear him.
   ☐ Everyone could hear him.
8. ☐ It was extremely difficult for her.
   ☐ It wasn't very hard for her.

B **Complete the sentences with the correct adverbs from the box.**

| clearly   quickly   fast   well   hard   slowly   ~~honestly~~   carefully |

1. Are you telling me the truth? I want you to speak ____honestly____ .
2. Catherine is a great tennis player. She plays very _____ .
3. This assignment is very short and won't take much time at all. You'll finish it fairly _____ .
4. Don't wait for me! I'm not a fast driver. I drive very _____ .
5. Sean wins every race. He runs really _____ .
6. Maria finished her project. She was up all night. She worked really _____ .
7. That engineer never makes mistakes. He always works _____ .
8. You are very easy to understand. You pronounce everything really _____ .

C **Rewrite the sentences and questions with adverbs instead of adjectives.**

1. Ana is a really careful driver.
   ____Ana drives really carefully____ .
2. Sam is an extremely fast swimmer.
   _____ .
3. Matthew is not a very hard worker.
   _____ .
4. Nicole is a fairly quick learner.
   _____ .
5. Jackson is a very careless writer.
   _____ .

6. Is John a good cook?
   ____Does John cook well____ ?
7. Is Diana a slow runner?
   _____ ?
8. Are you a very careful listener?
   _____ ?
9. Aren't the kids good singers?
   _____ ?
10. Is this an easy game to play?
    _____ ?

A ▶03-02 Listen to the sentences. Do they describe how someone feels or felt? Or do they describe someone or something that caused a feeling? Check (✓) the correct box.

	1	2	3	4	5	6	7	8
How someone feels or felt	✓							
Someone or something caused a feeling								

B Complete the sentences with the correct participial adjective form of the verbs in bold.

1. Mike's news **surprised** everyone.

   The news was _____surprising_____ .

   Everyone was _____surprised_____ by the news.

2. Angie's vacation was great. She was really able to **relax**.

   Angie's vacation was _____ .

   She felt _____ on her vacation.

3. The marketing job **interests** me.

   I am _____ in the marketing job.

   The marketing job sounds _____ .

4. That history class **bores** Sam.

   Sam is _____ in his history class.

   Sam thinks his history class is _____ .

5. The situation really **embarrassed** Eva.

   Eva found the situation really _____ .

   Eva was _____ by the situation.

6. We saw this story about doctors in Nepal last night. The story **fascinated** us.

   The story was _____ .

   We were _____ by the story.

C Complete the sentences with the *-ed* or *-ing* form of the verbs in parentheses.

1. There was a really _____embarrassing_____ situation at work this morning.
   (embarrass)
2. Chris has some _____ ideas.
   (interest)
3. The workers were _____ and needed a break.
   (tire)
4. Alex and Claire have some very _____ news.
   (excite)
5. Professor Lee is an _____ teacher. Everyone loves her classes.
   (amaze)
6. This is a _____ problem. I can't solve it.
   (confuse)
7. What is that _____ noise? It sounds like an alarm clock.
   (annoy)
8. Where is Michael? He wasn't in class all week. I'm a little _____ .
   (worry)

UNIT 3, LESSON 2   PRESENT PERFECT FOR PAST EXPERIENCES

A ▶03-09 Listen to the conversations. For each conversation, decide if the events happened at a specific time in the past or at an indefinite time in the past. Check (✓) the correct box.

	1	2	3	4	5	6	7
a specific time in the past							
an indefinite time in the past	✓						

B Complete the sentences with the present perfect or simple past form of the verbs in parentheses.

1. Elsie __has worked__ for several different companies. Last year, she _____had_____ a job
   (work)   **(have)**
   at a technology company.

2. Amira _____ to Argentina last month. She _____ a lot for her job this
            (go)   **(travel)**
   past year.

3. Last week, Dan _____ Germany. He _____ many trips to Europe for
                    (visit)   **(take)**
   work.

4. Thanks for the invitation, but I _____ lunch already. I _____ lunch a
                                    (eat)   **(eat)**
   couple of hours ago.

5. Laura _____ to many different countries, but she _____ in another
           (be)   **(not / live)**
   country.

6. _____ you _____ the news yet? Mario and Sofie _____
                      (hear)   **(get)**
   engaged last week.

7. I _____ that new Korean restaurant downtown. _____ you
      (not / try)
   _____ there yet?
      (be)

8. _____ you _____ Bill's report? He _____ a couple mistakes
                      (check)   **(make)**
   last time.

C Rewrite the paragraph to talk about Tyler's life sometime in the past. Change all the simple past verbs to the present perfect.

Last year, Tyler had several different jobs. He worked at a popular Japanese restaurant. He took some Japanese cooking classes. He even went to Japan, but he didn't learn Japanese. Tyler also lived in Mexico. He taught English classes and worked as a tour guide. He traveled to different Mexican cities and saw a lot of beautiful places. He met people from all over the world and made new friends. Tyler had some very interesting experiences.

Tyler has had several different jobs. _____

_____

_____

_____

_____

A ▶03-17 Listen to the sentences. Are the situations good or bad? Check (✓) the correct box.

	1	2	3	4	5	6	7	8
good	✓							
bad								

B Fill in the blanks with *could, couldn't,* or the correct form of *be able to*. More than one answer may be possible.

1. We <u>couldn't / weren't able to</u> complete our homework. We needed more time.
2. Malik _____ read when he was only four years old. His parents were very proud of him.
3. We _____ find Alice's house. Your directions were very clear.
4. Andrea hurt her leg. She _____ drive for three weeks.
5. Our dinner was delicious, but we _____ finish all the food.
6. When I was a child, I _____ speak French, but now I can't.
7. Ellen _____ fix her computer when it crashed this morning. She's great with computers.
8. Juan _____ play chess, but Gabi taught him.

C Write two sentences for each picture. Use *couldn't* in one sentence and *wasn't / weren't able to* in the other sentence.

1. (read / the newspaper) <u>He couldn't read the newspaper</u>.
   <u>He wasn't able to read the newspaper</u>.

2. (start / the car) _____.
   _____.

3. (lift / the box) _____.
   _____.

4. (play / outside) _____.
   _____.

5. (play / tennis) _____.
   _____.

6. (understand / the instructions) _____.
   _____.

UNIT 4, LESSON 1 COUNT AND NON-COUNT NOUNS WITH *SOME*, *ANY*, AND *NO*

A ▶04-02 Listen to the sentences. Fill in the missing words. Then read the sentences again and check (✓) whether the word in each blank is a count noun or a non-count noun.

	Count	Non-count
1. Where can I buy ___some apples___ ?	✓	
2. Do we have _____ ?		
3. Can you stop by the store? We have _____ .		
4. Would you like _____ ?		
5. There is _____ on this salad.		
6. I'm going to have _____ for lunch.		
7. Are there _____ in this building?		
8. There aren't _____ left.		

B Fill in the blanks with *some, any,* or *no.*

1. Do we have _____any_____ iced tea?
2. Michael is making _____ spinach and mushroom pasta.
3. We don't have _____ salad dressing.
4. Jo is a vegetarian. There are _____ vegetarian dishes on the menu. Let's go someplace else.
5. I really want Indian food, but there aren't _____ Indian restaurants nearby.
6. I need _____ water. It's hot and I'm thirsty!
7. I'm making _____ coffee. Would you like a cup?
8. This dessert tastes sweet, but it has _____ sugar in it.

C Complete the questions with *Is there/Are there any.* Complete the answers with *There is/ There are some,* or *There is/There are no.*

1. A: _____Is there any_____ ketchup?
   B: Yes, _____there is some_____ over there.
2. A: _____ burgers?
   B: No, _____ burgers left.
3. A: _____ restaurants in the airport?
   B: Yes, _____ on the second floor.
4. A: _____ seafood dishes? I really want fish tonight.
   B: _____ seafood dishes. Do you want to go somewhere else?
5. A: _____ coffee?
   B: _____ coffee, but there is some tea. Would you like a cup?
6. A: _____ forks? I see a lot of spoons, but no forks.
   B: Yes, _____ on that table in the corner.
7. A: _____ milk in this coffee?
   B: Yes, _____ milk in it. I can make one without milk.
8. A: _____ bread left? I want to make a sandwich.
   B: _____ bread left. We have to go to the store.

A ▶04-10 Listen to the sentences. Circle the correct answers to complete the responses.

1. How (much) / many do you need?
2. How *much / many* is he making?
3. How *much / many* should we make?
4. How *much / many* did they eat?
5. Sure, but I don't want *very much / too many*.
6. OK, but let's not order too *much / many*.
7. Yes, but I didn't add *very much / too many*.
8. How *much / many* cartons do we need?

B Complete the conversation with *much*, *many*, or *a lot of*. More than one answer may be possible.

A: You have ____a lot of____ ingredients here! What are you making?
   ₁

B: Cookies. Want to help?

A: Sure, but I don't have _____ time. How long will it take?
   ₂

B: Not long. Could you get me some flour and sugar, please?

A: OK. How _____ do you need?
   ₃

B: Two cups of each. Could you get some eggs from the fridge?

A: OK. How _____ do you need?
   ₄

B: Three. Could you pass the salt?

A: Uh-oh. We don't have _____ salt left.
   ₅

B: It's OK. I just need a little. There! Now let's put these in the oven.

A: How _____ minutes do they need to bake?
   ₆

B: About twenty four.

A: Mmm! They smell delicious. How _____ cookies are there?
   ₇

B: Thirty.

A: And how _____ people are coming over?
   ₈

B: Five or six. We'll have plenty of cookies left over!

C Look at the sentences. If possible, replace *a lot of* with *much* or *many*. If it's not possible, write *no change* after the sentence.

1. This cereal doesn't have ~~a lot of~~ sugar.   *much*

2. There aren't a lot of Japanese restaurants in this city.

3. Do you drink a lot of coffee in the morning?

4. Did you order a lot of food for the party?

5. This salad has a lot of different vegetables.

6. I eat a lot of soup in the winter.

7. The farmer's market has a lot of fruits and vegetables.

8. There is a lot of oil in this dish.

A ▶04-16 Listen to the conversations. Decide if they have *too much / many* or *enough / not enough*. Check (✓) the correct box.

	1. blueberries	2. seats	3. watermelons	4. tomatoes	5. sugar	6. bread	7. lemonade	8. honey
too much								
too many	✓							
enough								
not enough								

B Complete the sentences using *too much, too many,* or *enough*.

1. He can't make the cookies. He doesn't have _____enough_____ sugar.
2. He's really full. He ate _____ pizza.
3. The menu is six pages long. There are _____ choices.
4. She didn't have _____ time to go to a restaurant for lunch. So she ate at her desk.
5. She decided to order two desserts. There were _____ to choose from.
6. There are _____ sandwiches for everyone. Please help yourself.
7. She is eating _____ ice cream. She's going to have a stomachache.
8. We bought _____ apples. Let's make an apple pie.

C Rewrite the sentences.
Part I: Put the word *enough* in the correct place.

1. We don't have time for this recipe.
   We don't have enough time for this recipe   .

2. There are tomatoes for the salad.
   _____.

3. She has cookies for everyone.
   _____.

4. Do you have honey for your tea?
   _____?

5. Is there ice cream for everyone?
   _____?

Part II: Put the phrase *too much* or *too many* in the correct place.

6. This soup has salt in it.
   _____.

7. We bought hot dogs for the picnic.
   _____.

8. I ate cookies after dinner.
   _____.

9. Ben poured milk in his cereal.
   _____.

10. You put eggs in the bowl.
   _____.

UNIT 5, LESSON 1   *COULD* AND *SHOULD* FOR SUGGESTIONS

A ▶05-02 Listen to the conversations. Circle the correct answers.

1. You *should /* [*shouldn't*] leave your laptop there.
2. You *could / shouldn't* share your password with anyone.
3. You *could / couldn't* ask the receptionist for the correct name.
4. You *should / shouldn't* call her.
5. I *could / couldn't* show you how.
6. You *should / shouldn't* ask him.
7. She *could / shouldn't* use a new case.
8. I *could / shouldn't* give you a ride.

B Use *could, should,* or *shouldn't* and the verb in parentheses to complete the sentences. More than one answer may be possible.

1. A: My phone is really slow.

   B: Let me see. You have so many apps! You <u>shouldn't download</u> any more.
   (download)

2. A: My wireless network isn't working. I can't connect.

   B: You _____ Chris for help. He works in tech support.
   (call)

3. A: Kevin's presentation is at 9:00.

   B: We really _____ to his presentation. He's a great speaker!
   (go)

4. A: My dad emailed me a link to a website. I think I can win a prize if I click on it.

   B: You _____ on it! Call your dad. Someone might be using his email.
   (click)

5. A: _____ I _____ my laptop to the meeting?
   (bring)
   B: No, it really isn't necessary. You won't need to take notes or anything.

6. A: Where _____ I _____ my coat?
   (leave)
   B: You should probably take it with you. Don't leave it in the meeting room.

C Form statements or questions with the words in parentheses and *should, shouldn't,* or *could.*

1. A: I left my phone in the taxi. What should I do?

   B: _____<u>You should call the taxi company</u>_____ .
   (you, call the taxi company)

2. A: This app is from a company I've never heard of, and it doesn't have many reviews.

   B: _____ . It might not be safe.
   (you, download it)

3. A: I don't have time to finish my presentation.

   B: I have some time. _____ .
   (I, help you)

4. A: My computer is really slow. I can't open any files.

   B: _____ .
   (you, definitely restart it)

5. A: _____ ?
   (we, update our website)
   B: Yes, we should. Some of the links don't work.

6. A: _____ ?
   (Where, I, connect my computer)
   B: There's a spot in the conference room near the projector. Let me show you.

A ▶05-10 Listen to the sentences. Circle the correct answers.

1. Ana *will probably* / *will definitely* be late.
2. The coffee shop *might* / *probably won't* have free Wi Fi.
3. Chris *will* / *may* buy new headphones.
4. Restarting the computer *likely won't* / *might* fix the problem.
5. There *will* / *may* be a problem with Mai's hard drive.
6. Alicia *will* / *will probably* cancel their presentation.
7. John and Kirsten *will* / *might* have a video call soon.
8. Selena *may* / *will* have the wrong password.

B Read the sentences. Circle the correct answers.

1. The weather report says there's a 70 percent chance of rain tomorrow.
   a. It probably won't rain tomorrow.   b. It will probably rain tomorrow.
   c. It will definitely rain tomorrow.
2. Traffic is terrible this morning. I'll be at least thirty minutes late today.
   a. She might be late.   b. She will definitely be late.   c. She won't be late.
3. We don't need to give Ken directions. He has a GPS app on his phone.
   a. Ken will probably need directions.   b. Ken likely won't ask for directions.
   c. Ken will definitely ask for directions.
4. Why didn't you make a reservation? That restaurant is always very busy. I don't think we'll get a table.
   a. They might have a reservation.   b. They might not get a table.
   c. The restaurant won't likely be busy.
5. I should probably buy a new computer. My old one crashes all the time, and I don't think I can fix it.
   a. She will definitely fix her computer.   b. Her old computer won't likely crash again.
   c. She will likely get a new computer.
6. We should go to the meeting now. Let's not wait for Lucy. She's almost always late.
   a. They will wait for Lucy.   b. They might have a meeting.   c. Lucy will likely be late.

C Complete the sentences based on the situations. Use *will, won't,* or *might*.

1. John is working hard to get good grades in his classes. He has two more semesters left.
   _____He will_____ probably graduate next year.
2. Karen is thinking about moving to London. She isn't sure.
   _____ move to London.
3. Sam is driving from downtown. There was an accident there a few minutes ago.
   _____ likely be late.
4. My computer always crashes when I use this program.
   _____ probably crash again.
5. I'm not sure about going to see that movie. I don't usually watch action films.
   _____ see that movie.
6. Keith wants a new computer, but he can't afford one.
   _____ likely _____ buy a new computer.

A ▶05-13 Listen to the conversations. Circle the statements that are true.

1. a. Lily needs to meet Tim.   (b.) He doesn't have to introduce Tim.
2. a. He has to send Kevin an invitation.   b. Kevin doesn't need to be at the meeting.
3. a. She doesn't need to get drinks.   b. She doesn't have to order lunch.
4. a. She needs to reschedule.   b. She doesn't have to reserve a room.
5. a. He has to make more copies.   b. He didn't have to make so many copies.
6. a. Carlos needs to go to the presentation. b. Carlos doesn't have to speak Spanish.
7. a. She has to ask Claire for new headphones. b. She doesn't need to order new headphones.
8. a. He doesn't have to meet new clients.   b. He needs to be on time tomorrow.

B Complete the sentences with the correct form of *need to* or *have to*. More than one answer may be possible.

1. You <u>don't have to / don't need to</u> make photocopies. We can email it to everyone instead.
2. Sorry I'll be a little late. I _____ meet a new client at the downtown office this morning.
3. Thank you so much for buying my lunch! You _____ do that.
4. You _____ set up your webcam before our video call tomorrow. Do you need help with that?
5. James can't be here this afternoon. He _____ take his daughter to the doctor.
6. Maggie _____ work late tonight. She already finished her work.
7. _____ reserve a room for our presentation next week?
8. Laura's flight is very early. What time _____ leave?
9. Does Mike _____ write an agenda for the meeting? I think it would help to organize the meeting.

C Write questions using the correct form of *need to* or *have to* and the words in parentheses. More than one answer may be possible.

1. A: (Jack) _____ <u>Does Jack have to</u> _____ work late tonight?
   B: No, but he had to work late on Monday.
2. A: (I) _____ make a reservation for that restaurant?
   B: No, it's not necessary. They usually can seat you right away.
3. A: (she) _____ leave early yesterday?
   B: No, she didn't. Her appointment was canceled.
4. A: (What time, we) _____ be here tomorrow?
   B: No later than 7:00. The meeting starts at 7:15.
5. A: (When, you) _____ turn in your project?
   B: The deadline is next Friday.
6. A: (Why, Scott) _____ go to Korea?
   B: He is going to a conference in Seoul.
7. A: (Alice) _____ arrange a video call?
   B: No, she doesn't. The meeting was canceled.
8. A: (What, we) _____ bring to the conference?
   B: Bring a notebook and your I.D. badge.

UNIT 6, LESSON 1   *TOO* AND *ENOUGH* + ADJECTIVES

A ▶06-02 Listen to the conversations. Circle the correct answers.

1. The dressing *isn't sour enough* / (*is too sour*) / *isn't too sour*.
2. The cake *isn't big enough* / *is too big* / *isn't small enough*.
3. The coffee *is warm enough* / *is too cold* / *isn't cold enough*.
4. This soup *isn't salty enough* / *isn't rich enough* / *is too sweet*.
5. The cookies *aren't cool enough* / *are too cool* / *aren't hot enough* to eat.
6. It will be *cold enough* / *too cold* / *too hot* to have a picnic.
7. He's *old enough* / *too young* / *isn't too young* to work at the restaurant.

B Complete the sentences with *too* or *enough* plus the adjective in parentheses.

1. Do you think this soup is __warm enough__ to eat yet?
   (warm)
2. This dish is perfect! Don't add any salt. It's _____ .
   (salty)
3. I don't like the taste of dark chocolate. It's _____ .
   (bitter)
4. Can we wait a little before we eat dinner? I'm not _____ to eat yet.
   (hungry)
5. Let's eat somewhere else. It's hard to talk in here because the music is _____ .
   (loud)
6. Do you have some hot sauce? This food isn't _____ .
   (spicy)
7. We need to throw out this milk. It's old, and now it's _____ to drink.
   (sour)
8. Is your coffee _____ ? It looks a little light, and I know you love really
   (strong)
   dark coffee.
9. This cake is way _____ . I need a glass of milk.
   (sweet)
10. Can I get some ice? My drink isn't _____ .
    (cold)
11. Wait. Don't eat that yet. It just came out of the oven. It's _____ .
    (hot)

C Complete the sentences.
Part I: Complete the sentences using *too* + the boldfaced adjective.

1. Miriam is very **tired**. She *'s too tired* to cook dinner.
2. This food is very **spicy**. It _____ to eat.
3. Dan's very **busy** tonight. He _____ to go out.
4. This shelf is really **high**. It _____ for me to reach.
5. These onions are so **bitter**. They _____ to use.
6. This tea is really **cold**. It _____ to drink.

Part II: Complete the sentences using *enough* + the boldfaced adjective.

7. These strawberries are very **sweet**. They *'re sweet enough* to eat for dessert.
8. This dish is so **good**! It _____ for a dinner party.
9. That pot is very **large**. It _____ to make pasta.
10. That coffee isn't **hot**. It _____ to drink.
11. This pie is really **big**. It _____ for 12 people!
12. The green peppers aren't **spicy**. Use the red peppers instead. The red ones
    _____ for this recipe.

A ▶06-10 Listen to the conversations. Circle the true statement.

1. a. They got a card for Alice.
   b. Susie got a card from Alice.

2. a. She's cooking dinner for her family.
   b. Her family is cooking her dinner.

3. a. She's buying her parents a gift.
   b. Her parents bought her something silver.

4. a. Emma and Ryan gave her some flowers.
   b. She's giving flowers to Emma and Ryan.

5. a. She offered Tim a concert ticket.
   b. Tim gave her a concert ticket.

6. a. She gave her kids a book.
   b. She's going to read her kids a story.

7. a. She made her aunt a sweater.
   b. Her aunt made her a sweater.

8. a. She might buy her sister a suitcase.
   b. Her sister gave her a suitcase.

B Write sentences with the words.

1. cooked / dinner / I / my neighbors / for
   <u>I cooked dinner for my neighbors</u>   .

2. sent / a long letter / Jack / her

   _____ .

3. us / The waiter / brought / to / the food

   _____ .

4. the day off / Their boss / them / gave

   _____ .

5. me / Korean / Ms. Park / taught

   _____ .

6. I / my roommate / gave / to / some perfume

   _____ .

C Rewrite the sentences.
Part I. Rewrite the sentences so the indirect object is first.

1. Jorge bought a bike for his son.
   <u>Jorge bought his son a bike</u>   .

2. I got a diamond necklace for my wife.

   _____ .

3. Kylie found the perfect gift for her mother.

   _____ .

4. Tom brought some chocolate for his kids.

   _____ .

Part II. Rewrite the sentences so the direct object is first.

5. Trisha read her nephew a story.
   <u>Trisha read a story to her nephew</u>   .

6. I sent my best friend a funny birthday card.

   _____ .

7. Maya showed us her wedding pictures.

   _____ .

8. Jill made her co-workers some cookies.

   _____ .

PAST CONTINUOUS WITH *WHEN*

A ▶06-17 Listen. Complete the sentences with the past continuous.

1. Jane ___was traveling___ for business when she met her husband.
2. We _____ dinner when our neighbor unexpectedly stopped by.
3. _____ when I called?
4. _____ when you left this morning?
5. We took a taxi to work yesterday because the trains _____ .
6. Why _____ when Bob came in?
7. Where _____ when we saw her yesterday?

B Complete the sentences with the past continuous form of the verbs in the box.

| do   have   ~~leave~~   meet   play   shop   think |

1. I only saw Chris and Mary for a few minutes at the party. They ___were leaving___ by the time I got there.
2. I'm sorry I missed your call last night. I _____ dinner with some friends.
3. What _____ you _____ when you cut your hand?
4. I _____ about Ellen this morning. Have you talked to her lately?
5. I went to the park last night and I ran into Joan and Martin. They _____ tennis.
6. I _____ with some clients this afternoon so I didn't get a chance to see Paul.
7. _____ she _____ when you saw her at the mall?

C Use *when* to combine the two sentences. Use the simple past and the past continuous in each sentence.

1. First: I walked to the train.
   Second: I saw an old friend.
   _I was walking to the train when I saw an old friend_____.
2. First: They drove home.
   Second: They saw a terrible accident.
   _____.
3. First: Everyone ate dinner.
   Second: I got home.
   _____.
4. First: We had lunch.
   Second: The storm started.
   _____.
5. First: I watched a boring TV show.
   Second: I fell asleep.
   _____.
6. First: Tania didn't work yesterday.
   Second: I stopped by her office.
   _____.
7. First: Mike waited in line to buy tickets.
   Second: Someone offered him a free ticket.
   _____.

A ▶07-02 **Listen to the conversations. Complete each sentence with a preposition and gerund.**

1. They talked _____<u>about going</u>_____ to a North African restaurant.

2. Caroline is excited _____ a vacation with her family.

3. John is tired _____ for work.

4. Jennifer is looking forward _____ home.

5. Bruno is nervous _____ on a boat tour.

6. Maria thanked Susie _____ her.

7. Katie is interested _____ Amy's vacation pictures.

B **Match the sentence parts. Write the letter on the line.**

<u>e</u> 1. Sam and Ellen are excited   a. for buying our tickets.

___ 2. We were interested   b. of traveling to unusual places.

___ 3. Lin is worried   c. about missing her flight.

___ 4. I look forward   d. to it today.

___ 5. They aren't responsible   e. about visiting the pyramids.

___ 6. Dave isn't afraid   f. for your rude behavior.

___ 7. You need to apologize   g. to meeting you.

___ 8. She doesn't feel up   h. in going on a private tour.

C **Complete each sentence with the correct preposition and the gerund form of the verb in parentheses.**

A: Are you excited __<u>about going</u>__ on your road trip to the Canadian Rockies?
   1 (go)

B: Yes, I've been dreaming about this trip for a while. But I'm worried _____ lost.
   2 (get)
   The GPS doesn't always work.

A: You should think _____ an old-fashioned paper map.
   3 (buy)

B: We have some paper maps, but I'm not used _____ them.
   4 (read)

A: Right, I understand. I'm interested _____ the Canadian Rockies, but I don't want
   5 (visit)
   to drive. How many hours will you be in a car?

B: About twenty hours total.

A: That's crazy! Won't you get tired _____ ?
   6 (drive)

B: No, I don't think so. I love it! I really look forward _____ on the road. And
   7 (be)
   besides, we talked about getting a room if we feel tired.

A: Oh, OK. It doesn't sound fun to me, but I believe _____ new things. Maybe I'll
   8 (try)
   take a road trip for my next vacation.

B: You should! It's awesome. You'll thank me _____ it.
   9 (suggest)

A: OK. I'll let you know if I'm feeling up to it when I plan my next trip.

B: Sounds good.

A ▶07-10 Listen to the conversations. Circle the correct answers.

1. Yuki's parents would like / wouldn't like to see old buildings.
2. Mike *would love* / *wouldn't like* to go camping.
3. John *would love* / *wouldn't like* to eat Greek food.
4. Magda *would like* / *wouldn't like* to swim in Silver Lake.
5. Brenda *would like* / *would hate* to visit places that are not well known.
6. Sam *would love* / *wouldn't like* to go to a modern place.

B Complete the conversations with the correct form of the verb and infinitive. Use the words in parentheses.

1. A: What languages ____would you like to learn____ ?
      (you / would like / learn)
   B: I would love to speak Chinese.

2. A: Is Damien going to New York City for his vacation?
   B: I don't think so. He _____ somewhere crowded.
      (would hate / go)

3. A: My hometown isn't famous, but I love it. It's very safe and clean.
   B: It sounds nice. I _____ it someday.
      (would like / visit)

4. A: What do you want to do tonight?
   B: I _____ anything. Can we just stay home?
      (not want / do)

5. A: _____ a glass of water?
      (you / Would like / have)
   B: That would be great. Thanks.

6. A: What cities _____ ?
      (you / would like / visit)
   B: I'm not sure, but I usually like to go to places that are not well known.

7. A: Where _____ tonight?
      (you / want / eat / do)
   B: I don't care. Why don't you decide?

C Rewrite the sentences in bold using *would / wouldn't like*, *would love*, or *would hate*. More than one answer may be possible. Use contractions when possible.

1. **I really don't want to miss my flight.** The next flight isn't until tomorrow.
   I'd hate to miss my flight   .

2. Molly loves to travel. **She hopes to visit an ancient city someday.**
   _____ .

3. **We really want to see some famous tourist attractions.** We came to Paris for this reason.
   _____ .

4. **Charlie doesn't want to go to touristy places.** But he'll go if the whole group wants to go.
   _____ .

5. **I definitely don't want to be late for our tour.** I reserved our spots four months ago!
   _____ .

6. **Do you want to go to the modern art museum?**
   _____ ?

7. **Does your friend want to come with us?**
   _____ ?

8. **What cities do you want to visit?**
   _____ ?

A ▶07-15 Listen to the conversations. Then complete the sentences.

1. Mt. Everest is _____ taller _____ than Mt. Kilimanjaro.
2. The Caspian Sea is the _____ lake in the world.
3. He thinks that lakes are _____ than ponds.
4. The Sahara Desert is the _____ desert.
5. The hotels on the coast are the _____ hotels in the city.
6. Calgary, Canada is the _____ city in the world.

B Complete the sentences with the correct form of the adjectives in parentheses.

Dubai and Abu Dhabi are two of the _most famous_ cities in the United Arab Emirates.
1 (famous)

Dubai is the _____ city in the country. With its tall skyscrapers, Dubai is possibly
2 (big)

the _____ city in the Middle East. In fact, the _____ skyscraper in the
3 (modern)   4 (high)

world, the Burj Khalifa, is located in Dubai. Abu Dhabi is older and _____ than
5 (traditional)

Dubai. The average temperature in Abu Dhabi is 96°F, but Dubai is a little _____ ,
6 (hot)

with an average temperature of 104°F. While Dubai is modern, many people prefer Abu

Dhabi because it is _____ than Dubai.
7 (expensive)

C Look at the chart. Write sentences with comparatives and superlatives using the given adjectives. More than one answer may be possible.

	Mexico City, Mexico	Warsaw, Poland	Hanoi, Vietnam
Population	8.851 million	1.735 million	7.6 million
Area	573 km²	517 km²	3,329 km²
Average temperature	17°C	16°C	31°C
Year founded	1521	1200	1010

1. *big (in population)*
   comparative: Hanoi is bigger than Warsaw _____.
   superlative: Mexico City is the biggest city _____.
2. *large (in area)*
   comparative: _____.
   superlative: _____.
3. *cold*
   comparative: _____.
   superlative: _____.
4. *old*
   comparative: _____.
   superlative: _____.

A ▶08-03 Listen to the questions. Circle the correct responses.

1. a. He's a drummer.   b. Joe plays drums.
2. a. Bianca plays instruments.   b. She plays the violin, guitar, and piano.
3. a. I'm listening to a new rock band.   b. I'm listening to the radio.
4. a. Max is wearing the green jacket.   b. The green jacket is Max's.
5. a. That song is so sad.   b. The Clouds sing that song.
6. a. Ari is a bassist.   b. It's a person who plays a bass instrument.
7. a. Pete Ross is the guitarist.   b. That band has a guitarist.
8. a. He plays the saxophone.   b. He plays with that jazz band.

B Complete the conversations. Make questions using the information from Speaker B.

1. A: What instruments _____do you play_____?
   B: I play the violin and guitar.
2. A: What time _____ to the concert?
   B: She's going at 8:00.
3. A: Who _____ the bassist?
   B: John Tibbs.
4. A: What instrument _____?
   B: Jae plays the trumpet.
5. A: What kind of music _____?
   B: I like rock music.
6. A: What band _____ at the park last night?
   B: A new jazz band performed at the park.
7. A: Who _____ for that band?
   B: Ray Jones sings for that band.
8. A: What kind of music lessons _____ when you were young?
   B: I took violin lessons in high school.

C Change the sentences to questions. The words in bold should be the answers to the questions you make.

1. Jake went **to a concert** last weekend.
   What did Jake do last weekend ?
2. His name is **Michael**.
   _____ ?
3. Sue plays **the keyboard**.
   _____ ?
4. I saw **Talking Hearts** in concert.
   _____ ?
5. **Kamila** knocked on the door.
   _____ ?
6. Emma taught **piano lessons**.
   _____ ?
7. **Darren** taught drum lessons.
   _____ ?

UNIT 8, LESSON 2   *SO / BECAUSE (OF) TO SHOW CAUSE AND EFFECT*

A ▶08-11 Listen to the conversations. Circle the correct statements.

1. (a.) They're going to the game because it's the last game of the season.
   b. They're going to miss the game, so they'll go to another one next spring.
2. a. She wants to go to the art gallery because there's a new art show.
   b. They didn't go to the art gallery last weekend, so they'll go tonight.
3. a. There aren't any musicals, so they'll go to a comedy club instead.
   b. Because she doesn't like musicals, they'll do something else instead.
4. a. He offered her a ticket because she's never been to the ballet.
   b. He had an extra ticket, so he offered it to her.
5. a. Tickets are sold out, so they can't go to the opera.
   b. They're going to the opera because they bought their tickets weeks ago.
6. a. The movie was scary, so she really didn't enjoy it.
   b. She didn't like the movie because of the actors.
7. a. They missed the whole show because they were stuck in traffic.
   b. They were stuck in traffic, so they missed half of the show.

B Complete the sentences with *so, because,* or *because of.*

1. We can't go to the art gallery tonight ____because____ it isn't open.
2. We're going to be late to the ballet _____ the heavy traffic.
3. The game was canceled last night, _____ we went to a movie instead.
4. I don't usually get popcorn at the movies _____ it's too salty.
5. My children love the opera _____ the fancy costumes.
6. Kelly loves to laugh, _____ let's take her to the comedy club for her birthday.
7. We didn't like the movie very much _____ the plot was really boring.
8. _____ the rain, the outdoor concert will probably be canceled.

C Write sentences using *so, because,* or *because of.*

1. The musical is sold out. We can't go.
   so: _The musical is sold out, so we can't go_____.
   because: _We can't go to the musical because it is sold out_____.
2. We loved the movie. The actors were amazing.
   because: _____.
   because of: _____.
3. We're going to a show this weekend. Scott's favorite band is performing.
   because: _____.
   so: _____.
4. I enjoyed the art gallery. The exhibit was very interesting.
   because: _____.
   because of: _____.
5. The opera tickets were too expensive. We saw a movie.
   because: _____.
   so: _____.

A ▶08-18 Listen to the conversations. Circle the correct answers.

1. Alex goes to the gym *every day* / *three days a week* / *several times* a day.
2. The exercise group runs *weekly* / *on weekends* / *five days a week*.
3. She spends time outdoors *all week* / *several times a week* / *on weekends*.
4. He turns off his phone *every morning* / *every night* / *24 hours a day*.
5. He told her to follow a balanced diet *on weekends* / *during the week* / *daily*.
6. She used to meditate *daily* / *weekly* / *monthly*, but now she meditates *every morning* / *once in a while* / *on weekends*.

B Write complete sentences to answer the questions. Use the information in parentheses.

1. Q: How often do you get a check-up? (once a year)
   A: I get a check up once a year   .

2. Q: When do you have practice? (in the evening)
   A: _____ .

3. Q: What days do you go to the gym? (Tuesdays and Thursdays)
   A: _____ .

4. Q: When do you spend time outdoors? (weekends)
   A: _____ .

5. Q: How often do you put down your device? (a few hours a day)
   A: _____ .

6. Q: How much do you sleep? (eight hours a night)
   A: _____ .

C Look at Maria's weekly planner. Use the words in parentheses to write sentences. Use each activity only one time.

	Monday	Tuesday	Wednesday	Thursday	Friday	Saturday	Sunday
6:00 AM	------------------------------- meditate (Monday–Sunday) -------------------------------						
8:00 AM – 5:00 PM	work at office			work at home		spend time outdoors	do volunteer work
6:00 PM	go to the gym	go to guitar lessons	go to the gym		go to a cooking class	go out with friends	

1. _____ She does volunteer work on Sundays _____ .
   (on Sundays)
2. _____ .
   (daily)
3. _____ .
   (on Mondays and Wednesdays)
4. _____ .
   (on Friday evenings)
5. _____ .
   (twice a week)
6. _____ .
   (three days a week)
7. _____ .
   (every Saturday)
8. _____ .
   (on weekends)
9. _____ .
   (on Tuesday evenings)

A ▶09-03 Listen to the questions. Circle the correct responses.

1. (a.) I'll help you.
   b. I'm going to help you.
2. a. It leaves at 7:00.
   b. My train will leave at 7:00.
3. a. Sure, I'm going to take it.
   b. Sure, I'll take it.
4. a. I'll make some new curtains.
   b. I'm going to make some new curtains.
5. a. Sure. I'll get one at the store today.
   b. Sure. I'm going to get one at the store.
6. a. I'm going to buy a new bookcase this weekend.
   b. I'll buy a new bookcase this weekend.

B Rewrite the sentences using the verb form in parentheses. Change the underlined word(s) to *tomorrow*.

1. My favorite TV show came on at 8:00 last night.
   (*simple present*) My favorite TV show comes on at 8:00 tomorrow night .
2. I bought a new couch yesterday.
   (*be going to*) _____ .
3. Lena sold her old rug and armchair last week.
   (*present continuous*) _____ .
4. I helped you move your furniture this morning.
   (*will*) _____ .
5. Dan's brother moved in with him last month.
   (*be going to*) _____ .
6. Joe started his new job yesterday.
   (*simple present*) _____ .
7. Eva looked for a new apartment last week.
   (*will*) _____ .

C Complete the conversation with *will*, *be going to*, the present continuous, or the simple present and the verb in parentheses.

A: What _____are you doing_____ after work today?
        1 (do)

B: I _____ Sandy move some furniture. She just moved into your building.
   2 (help)

A: I know! _____ to her apartment right after work? Can I get a ride with you?
      3 (go)

B: Sure, I _____ you a ride. I _____ when I get off work,
     4 (give)   **5 (leave)**
around 5:00 or 5:30. Is that OK with you?

A: Oh, today is Monday. I _____ off work at 6:00 on Mondays, but I
                     6 (get)
_____ if I can leave a little early.
   7 (see)

B: No, that's OK. I _____ until 6:00 for you.
          8 (wait)

A: Great! Thanks!

A ▶09-09 Listen. Circle the direct question that matches.

1. a. Why does James have to work late?
   b. Does James have to work late?

2. a. Where did everyone go?
   b. Did everyone go?

3. a. What time does the meeting start?
   b. Is the meeting starting now?

4. a. Where is Luisa today?
   b. Is Luisa in the office today?

5. a. Is the train delayed?
   b. Where is the train?

6. a. Did I lose my keys?
   b. Where did I put my keys?

B Write sentences and questions using the words in parentheses.

1. I think Maya has an apartment around here. _____I wonder where she lives_____ .
   (wonder / she / lives)

2. That man is waving at me, but I don't know him. _____ ?
   (do you know / he / is)

3. Liza's car looks really bad. The lights are falling off! _____ .
   (wonder / she / got into an accident)

4. I'm not familiar with this building. _____ ?
   (can you tell me / restroom / is)

5. There's a meeting tomorrow morning. _____ ?
   (do you know / we / are meeting)

6. I can't find my keys! _____ .
   (wonder / I / left them)

7. I need the report. _____ ?
   (could you tell me / it / is ready)

8. I need to go to the bank today. _____ .
   (I wonder / it / is open)

C Change the direct questions to indirect questions.
Part I. Begin each sentence with *I wonder*.

1. Where is Katie?
   I wonder where Katie is _____ .

2. What country is Maya from?
   _____ .

3. Do we have to work late tonight?
   _____ .

4. Did Jane lose her keys?
   _____ .

5. Why did Eric leave?
   _____ .

Part II. Begin each sentence with *Do you know*.

6. What did Peter say?
   _____ ?

7. What time did Alan leave last night?
   _____ ?

8. Was the train delayed?
   _____ ?

9. Did Dina get stuck in traffic?
   _____ ?

10. Where is Kelly today?
    _____ ?

A ▶09-16 Listen. Complete the sentences.

1. I think they're ___in the bedroom upstairs___ .

2. It's way too cold _____ !

3. It's _____ .

4. I'll see if there's a coffee shop _____ .

5. He's _____ .

6. Do you want to eat _____ ?

B Complete the sentences with the correct adverbial phrases from the box.

> in the backyard   at home   on the bookshelf   ~~in the kitchen~~   in the country
> at the office   on the table   in the middle

1. Jorge is ___in the kitchen___ cooking dinner.

2. Could you please put this book _____ ?

3. Oh, no. I left my umbrella _____ . Now I'm going to get wet.

4. I can't find my cat. I wonder if he's _____ .

5. Jack forgot his laptop _____ . He needs to go back to work.

6. There are some apples _____ .

7. They bought a beautiful house _____ .

8. Mary left her toy _____ of the yard.

C Rewrite each sentence. Add the adverb of place in parentheses.

1. I can't find my keys in the house. (anywhere)
   <u>I can't find my keys anywhere in the house</u> .

2. They're doing laundry in the basement. (downstairs)

   _____ .

3. Pat is working in the garden. (outside)

   _____ .

4. There is a café in this building. (somewhere)

   _____ .

5. I found some old pictures in the bedroom. (upstairs)

   _____ .

6. I don't know where I left my phone, but it's somewhere. (nearby)

   _____ .

7. Ann is eating in the kitchen. (inside)

   _____ .

A ▶10-02 **Listen. What does the speaker think is true? Circle the correct answers.**

1. a. They have a new designer on their team. b. They don't have a new designer on their team.
2. a. There are some open positions. b. There are no open positions.
3. a. Lisa is a manager. b. Lisa isn't a manager.
4. a. I can use Jim as a reference. b. I can't use Jim as a reference.
5. a. She was a candidate for the management position. b. She wasn't a candidate for the management position.
6. a. We're interviewing candidates next week. b. We aren't interviewing candidates next week.
7. a. Greg worked in Human Resources. b. Greg didn't work in Human Resources.

B **Complete the tag questions with the correct verbs.**

1. Kenji isn't in his office, _____is_____ he?
2. You submitted an application online, _____ you?
3. She's applying for another job, _____ she?
4. I don't need to include a cover letter with my résumé, _____ I?
5. They have an opening for a manager position, _____ they?
6. You can't be here an hour early tomorrow, _____ you?
7. He's applied for a position at our company before, _____ he?
8. We should hire someone who speaks Spanish, _____ we?
9. You don't have a pen I can borrow, _____ you?

C **Add a tag question to each conversation.**

1. A: Beatriz works in the Human Resources department, __doesn't she__ ?
   B: That's right. She's worked there for several years.
2. A: You're here to interview for the sales position, _____ ?
   B: No, I'm here for a sales meeting.
3. A: Hurry up! We're going to be late.
   B: Late for what? We don't have another meeting today, _____ ?
4. A: You haven't heard from Julie lately, _____ ?
   B: No, I haven't. I wonder what she's doing these days.
5. A: Did Gabe get the manager position?
   B: No. He wasn't even a candidate, _____ ?
6. A: This application has old information on it.
   B: We're going to update it, _____ ?
7. A: Your résumé looks great, but you forgot to include the languages you speak.
   B: Oh, that's right! I should include that, _____ ?
8. A: You'll apply for the new manager position, _____ ?
   B: No, I don't think so. I'm happy with my job now.
9. A: We need another person on the project. We can hire someone now, _____ ?
   B: No, we don't have the budget to hire anyone new this year.
10. A: You're starting your new job next week, _____ ?
    B: Yes, I am. I'm excited but also a little nervous.

A ▶10-10 Listen. Is the speaker talking about how long something lasted, when something started, or something that happened at a specific time in the past? Check (✓) the correct box.

	1	2	3	4	5	6	7
how long something lasted	✓						
when something started							
something that happened at a specific time in the past							

B Complete the sentences and questions with *for* and *since*.

1. We have worked on the budget _____for_____ over a week.
2. I've been here _____since_____ 6:00 this morning.
3. We haven't seen Chang _____ several weeks.
4. Rob has worked at the company _____ 2014.
5. Dylan hasn't given a presentation _____ the beginning of the year.
6. Tim and I have known each other _____ college.
7. Ali has had a cold _____ over a week.
8. Mario hasn't managed a team _____ last year.
9. Harry and Janice have been married _____ forty years.
10. I've been here _____ about an hour.
11. Have you eaten anything _____ this morning?
12. Has anyone seen Sam _____ Monday?

C Rewrite the sentences. Use the present perfect form of the verb and *for* or *since*.

1. I manage a large team. I began one month ago.
   <u>I have managed a large team for one month</u>   .
2. John works on the sales team. He started over a year ago.
   _____ .
3. I am done with my project. I finished it last night.
   _____ .
4. I know Karen. We met in March.
   _____ .
5. Luke is at the office. He got there at 6:00 this morning.
   _____ .
6. Brad lives in India. He moved there six months ago.
   _____ .
7. Ann is sick. She got sick on Tuesday.
   _____ .
8. I work in sales. I started three years ago.
   _____ .
9. Tom is in China. He arrived there last week.
   _____ .
10. John is unemployed. He quit his job in 2017.
    _____ .

A ▶10-17 **Listen. Complete the questions.**

1. _____ What have they _____ changed?
2. _____ happened?
3. _____ before?
4. So, _____ to him yet?
5. _____ open?
6. Terrific. _____ so far?
7. _____ ?

B **Complete the questions with the present perfect form of the words in parentheses.**

A: Why _____ have you applied _____ for this position?
  1 (you / apply)

B: I work for a small start-up company with only twenty employees, but I'd like to work for a larger company. Your company would be the perfect fit for me.

A: How long _____ interested in computer programming?
  2 (you / be)

B: I've always loved computers for as long as I can remember.

A: What companies _____ for in the past?
  3 (you / work)

B: I've worked for a couple of small technology companies.

A: In this position, you'll need to manage a small team. How _____
  4 (you / show)
  leadership at your other jobs?

B: At my current job, I manage a team of eight workers.

A: How _____ with conflict?
  5 (you / deal)

B: When a conflict comes up, I stay calm and work with my team to resolve the issue quickly.

A: Do you have any questions for me?

B: Yes. What challenges _____ in the past year?
  6 (the company / handle)

A: Our biggest challenge has been growth. We grew by over 2,000 employees last year.

B: How _____ the work environment?
  7 (this growth / change)

A: It's still a great place to work, but we've had to hire more people and find bigger offices.

C **Write questions in the present perfect using the words below.**

1. When / you / deal / with a conflict
   When have you dealt with a conflict _____ ?

2. How / she / handle / challenges
   _____ ?

3. Where / he / work / in the past
   _____ ?

4. When / you / think / outside the box
   _____ ?

5. How long / they / work / as a team
   _____ ?

6. How many calls / the assistant / answer / this morning
   _____ ?

7. What countries / you / visited / this past year
   _____ ?

VOCABULARY PRACTICE

UNIT 1, LESSON 4

Complete the sentences with words from the box.

workplace	research	encourage	friendship	employees

1. The teacher liked Lin's history paper because his _____ about the subject was excellent.
2. The company hired many new _____ when it opened the new factory.
3. Raffy and Tino began their _____ when they were in high school.
4. It is important for teachers to _____ students to do their best.
5. The _____ is made up of people from different places and experiences.

UNIT 2, LESSON 4

Complete the sentences with words from the box.

piece of advice	product	recycled	wise	elegant	designer

1. I always listen to my grandfather because he is such a _____ man.
2. The _____ made a beautiful drawing of a new dress.
3. Companies often advertise a new _____ on TV.
4. Soda cans and newspapers are often _____.
5. The movie star was wearing an _____ dress.
6. My teacher gave me a _____. She told me to make many mistakes and to be proud of them.

UNIT 3, LESSON 4

Complete the sentences with words from the box.

adrenaline rush	risk-taker	in control	out of control	fear	focus	flight

1. Trish doesn't like surprises and always wants to be _____.
2. The car hit a wall because it was _____.
3. I love how I feel when I skydive. It gives me such an _____.
4. I don't like most insects, and I have a terrible _____ of snakes!
5. I can't believe he jumped out of an airplane. He's a real _____.
6. Peter really needs to _____ on his work. His paper is due tomorrow!
7. Mario took a _____ from Mexico City to Paris yesterday.

UNIT 4, LESSON 4

Circle the correct answers.

1. When you get used to a kind of food, you **are unsure of it / dislike it / are comfortable with it**.
2. When someone has room for more food, they **are full / could eat more / need to go shopping**.
3. An example of a sweet treat is a **steak / salad / cake**.
4. When you relax your body, you make it **straight / loose / strong**.
5. When someone feels pleasure from a meal, they **enjoy it / don't like it / aren't satisfied**.
6. Someone who is having a bite of food is **cooking / eating / drinking**.
7. When you are satisfied by a meal, you are **upset / hungry / pleased**.
8. When something is expanded, it gets **bigger / heavier / tighter**.
9. A person can push open a **door / car / tree**.
10. The taste of sugar is **cold / hard / sweet**.

UNIT 5, LESSON 4

Match each word with its definition. Write the letter on the line.

___	1. three-dimensional	a.	the body part in your chest that makes blood move through your body
___	2. a disaster	b.	the smallest part that forms an animal or plant
___	3. waste	c.	materials from nature, such as land, forests, water, etc.
___	4. natural resources	d.	an event that causes great harm and damage, like a terrible storm
___	5. skin	e.	the body part in your chest that you use to breathe
___	6. organs	f.	what is left after you have used something
___	7. the lungs	g.	the outside part of a person's or animal's body
___	8. the heart	h.	parts of the body that have a special purpose
___	9. a cell	i.	with length, depth, and height

UNIT 6, LESSON 4

Circle the correct answers.

1. One word used to describe a cliff might be ___.
    a. soft
    b. flat
    c. high
2. An example of wildlife is ___.
    a. a cow on a farm
    b. a tiger in a desert
    c. a pet dog in a home
3. Someone in a cave is ___.
    a. inside a hole in a mountain
    b. outside on the edge of a mountain
    c. on top of a mountain
4. Limestone is ___.
    a. a type of water
    b. a type of rock
    c. a type of sand
5. A crane is often used to ___.
    a. build buildings
    b. pick vegetables
    c. make computers
6. A platform is ___.
    a. a raised area that people stand or sit on
    b. a machine used to carry large objects
    c. a place where boats are kept

UNIT 7, LESSON 4

Complete the sentences with words from the box.

| tank | submerged | palace | rules | butler | out of sight | faces | lick | rotate |

1. The king lived in a beautiful _____ with many rooms.
2. Every day, my puppy jumps up on me to _____ my face!
3. The wheels on a bicycle _____ so that it can move forward and backward.
4. I have a pet fish that lives in a _____ of water.
5. She is so lucky! She has a _____ to help take care of her house.
6. Frank's clothes were in the closet and _____ after he cleaned his room.
7. My building _____ the ocean. I can see the waves and the sand from my living room windows.
8. The plants grow out of the sand in the ocean. They're completely _____.
9. This game has _____ that the players have to follow.

UNIT 8, LESSON 4

Match each word group with a word. Write the letter on the line.

___ 1. brain, endorphin, body   a. stress
___ 2. beat, heart rate, repeated sound   b. piece
___ 3. worry, tension, pressure   c. translate
___ 4. emotion, feeling, attitude   d. hormone
___ 5. drawing, statue, painting   e. release
___ 6. change, turn, remake   f. mood
___ 7. let go, unleash, free up   g. rhythm

UNIT 9, LESSON 4

Complete the sentences with words from the box.

| used | directly | search engine | goods | browsing | dropdown menu |

1. I gave my homework _____ to the teacher at the start of the class. I didn't email it to her.
2. Frank clicked on the _____ to find the page that tells you about the company.
3. I typed "how to find free furniture" in the _____ and thousands of websites were listed.
4. I was _____ through pictures of furniture when I saw the perfect couch for my apartment!
5. This store sells furniture and other _____ for the home.
6. Susan didn't have enough money to buy a new computer, so she bought a _____ one.

Circle the correct answers.

1. Tina kept fidgeting; she couldn't ___.
   a. stay awake
   b. stop moving
   c. stop relaxing
2. When you convince a person, you want them to ___ what you say.
   a. question
   b. believe
   c. follow
3. An impressive job candidate is someone who has the ___.
   a. right skills
   b. best clothes
   c. most questions
4. A person who mumbles is ___.
   a. yelling loudly
   b. crying softly
   c. speaking quietly
5. When someone gives you a tip on how to do something, they give you ___.
   a. money
   b. advice
   c. a job
6. Rosa ___ as she slouched in the chair.
   a. stood up
   b. bent forward
   c. straightened up
7. Someone with a positive attitude shows that he or she is ___ something.
   a. happy about
   b. sad about
   c. tired of
8. Sam's body language was clear; his ___ told us exactly how he felt!
   a. words
   b. movements
   c. sounds

REFERENCES

UNIT 1, LESSON 1 PRESENT CONTINUOUS: STATEMENTS AND QUESTIONS

Affirmative statements

Subject	*Be*	Verb + *-ing*
I	am	
We They	are	talking.
He	is	

Negative statements

Subject	*Be*	Not	Verb + *-ing*
I	'm		
We They	're	not	talking.
He	's		

Yes/no questions

Be	Subject	Verb + *-ing*
Are	you	
Are	they	working?
Is	he	

Short answers

Affirmative	Negative
Yes, I **am**.	No, I**'m not**.
Yes, they **are**.	No, they **aren't**. / No, they**'re not**.
Yes, he **is**.	No, he **isn't**. / No, he**'s not**.

Wh- questions

Wh- word	*Be*	Subject	Verb + *-ing*
What	are	you	**doing**?
Where	is	he	**going**?
Who	are	you	**talking** to?
Why		they	**running**?

Answers

I'm fixing the computer.
He's going to work.
I'm talking to Jen.
Because they are late.

UNIT 1, LESSON 2 SIMPLE PAST, REGULAR VERBS: REVIEW

Affirmative statements

Subject	Verb	
I She	**visited**	Miami.
	watched	the sunset.

Negative statements

Subject	*Did + not*	Verb	
I She We	**did not**	**like**	the beaches.

Notes
- We almost always use the contraction *didn't* in speech and informal writing.

Spelling rules for regular verbs
- For most verbs, add *-ed* to the base form.   enjoy ➔ enjoy**ed**   walk ➔ walk**ed**
- For verbs that end in *e*, add only *d*.   lik**e** ➔ lik**ed**   lov**e** ➔ lov**ed**
- For verbs that end in a consonant + *y*, change the *y* to *i* and add *-ed*.
  stu**dy** ➔ stud**ied**   **try** ➔ tr**ied**
- For most verbs that end in consonant + vowel + consonant, double the last letter.
  s**top** ➔ sto**pped**   pl**an** ➔ pla**nned**

UNIT 1, LESSON 2   SIMPLE PAST, IRREGULAR VERBS: REVIEW

Affirmative statements		
Subject	**Verb**	
I	**ate**	at a restaurant.
She	**swam**	at the beach.
We	**got**	a massage.

Negative statements			
Subject	***Did + not***	**Verb**	
I		**eat**	at the hotel.
She	**did not**	**swim**	in the pool.
We		**get**	a double room.

Note: We almost always use the contraction *didn't* in speech and informal writing.

Common irregular verbs			
Base form	Simple past	Base form	Simple past
be	was, were	see	saw
buy	bought	sit	sat
go	went	sleep	slept
hang out	hung out	spend	spent
have	had	take	took
make	made	write	wrote

UNIT 1, LESSON 2   SIMPLE PAST QUESTIONS, REGULAR AND IRREGULAR VERBS: REVIEW

Yes / no questions				Short answers	
Did	**Subject**	**Verb**		**Affirmative**	**Negative**
Did	you	**learn**	English at school?	Yes, I **did.**	No, I **didn't.**
	she	**grow up**	in New York?	Yes, she **did.**	No, she **didn't.**

Information questions					Answers
***Wh-* word**	***Did***	**Subject**	**Verb**		
When		he	**start**	working?	In 2015.
Where	**did**	they	**get**	married?	In Bogotá.
Why		you	**move**	to Brazil?	For work.

Notes
- We almost always use the contraction *didn't*.
- To ask questions with *born*, you can say *Where were you born?* or *Were you born in New York?*

UNIT 2, LESSON 3   ADVERBS OF FREQUENCY

Statements with most verbs			
Subject	Adverb	Verb	
I	**always**	**get up**	early.
She	**rarely**	**gets up**	late.

Statements with *be*			
Subject	*Be*	**Adverb**	
I	**am**	**never**	late for
She	**is**	**sometimes**	work.

Yes / No questions with most verbs				
Do / Does	Subject	Adverb	Verb	
Do	you	**often**	**go**	to the
Does	he	**ever**		gym?

Yes / No questions with *be*			
Be	Subject	Adverb	
Are	you	**often**	late for
Is	he	**ever**	work?

Notes

- Use adverbs of frequency with simple present verbs, not present continuous verbs.
  It's 6:00 P.M., and Kate is ordering takeout. She **often orders** takeout for dinner.
- With *be*, put the adverb after *be* in statements and after the subject in questions.
  They **are never** late.   Are **they ever** late?
- With most verbs, put the adverb before the verb.
  They **always arrive** on time.
- Use *ever* in *yes / no* questions and negative statements only.
  Do not use *never* in questions.
  He **doesn't ever** stay up late. = He **never stays** up late.
  Does he **ever** stay up late? NOT Does he ~~never~~ stay up late?
- Do not use *sometimes, rarely,* or *never* in sentences with *not.*
- We almost always use contractions in speech and informal writing.

100%	**always**
	almost always
	usually
50%	**often**
	sometimes
	rarely / almost never
0%	**never**

UNIT 4, LESSON 1   *SOME / ANY* WITH COUNT AND NON-COUNT NOUNS: REVIEW

Statements				Yes/No questions			
Affirmative	I added	**some**	milk.	Do we need		any	milk?
Negative	I didn't add	any	eggs.			some	eggs?

Notes

- Don't use *some* or *any* when speaking about something in general.
  A: I love **fruit**! What about you?
  Do you like **fruit**?
  B: Yes, but I don't like **cherries**.
- Using *some* makes offers and requests sound more natural.
  A: Do you want **some** soda? Or **some** cookies?
  B: No, thanks, but can I have **some** water?

- You can use *some* and *any* alone when the meaning is clear.
  A: I made coffee. Do you want **some**?
  B: Thank you, but no, I don't want **any** right now.
- Remember, you can use *there + be + no +* noun.
  There's **no sugar**. = There isn't any sugar.
  There are **no cherries**. = There aren't any cherries.

UNIT 4, LESSON 2   QUESTIONS WITH *HOW MUCH* AND *HOW MANY*

How much	Non-count noun		Answers	How many	Plural noun		Answers
How much	bread	do we need?	A lot.	**How many**	vegetables	will there be?	Four.
	cheese		Not much.		desserts		Two.
	rice		Three bags.		people		Not many.

UNIT 7, LESSON 3   COMPARATIVE ADJECTIVES: REGULAR AND IRREGULAR

Use comparative adjectives to compare two people or things.

	Adjective	Comparative adjective
For most one-syllable adjectives, add *-(e)r* for the comparative.	fast	fast**er**
	cheap	cheap**er**
For one-syllable adjectives ending in one vowel + one consonant, double the final consonant and add *-er.*	thin	thin**ner**
	big	big**ger**
For two-syllable adjectives ending in *y*, drop the *y* and add *-ier*.	easy	eas**ier**
	dirty	dirt**ier**
For most adjectives with two or more syllables, use *more / less* + the adjective.	expensive	**more** expensive
	interesting	**less** interesting

Notes
- Use *than* when you use a comparative adjective in front of a noun.
  Laptops are more expensive **than tablets**.
- Some adjectives have irregular forms: good → **better**   bad → **worse**

UNIT 9, LESSON 1   *WILL* FOR FUTURE INTENTION

Affirmative statements			Negative statements			Yes / no questions			Short answers	
Subject	*Will*	**Verb**	**Subject**	*Will + not*	**Verb**	*Will*	**Subject**	**Verb**	**Affirmative**	**Negative**
I	will	wait.	I	will not	wait.	Will	he	come?	Yes, he will.	No, he won't.
We			We							

Information questions					Short answers
Wh- word	*Will*	**Subject**	**Verb**		
When	will	I	**see**	you?	After work.
What time		he	**get**	here?	At 10:00.

Notes
- You can use *will* + the base form of a verb to make an offer or state a plan made at the moment of speaking.
  A: I don't have a ride.   A: **I'll be** back in a minute.
  B: **I'll pick** you up.   B: Hurry! The movie **is** starting**.**
- We almost always contract the subject pronoun + *will* in speaking and informal writing.
  I will → **I'll**   they will → **they'll**   it will not → it **won't**   we will not → we **won't**
- Use contractions in negative short answers only.
  A: Will he call us back?   B: Yes, he **will**. / No, he **won't**.   NOT Yes, ~~he'll~~.

UNIT 9, LESSON 1   FUTURE PLANS WITH *BE GOING TO*

Affirmative statements					Negative statements				
Subject	*Be*	*Going to*	Base form of the verb		Subject	*Be + not*	*Going to*	Base form of the verb	
I	am				I	am not			
She	is	going to	start	college.	She	is not	going to	get	married.
We	are				We	are not			

Yes / *no* questions					Short answers		
Be	Subject	*Going to*	Verb		**Affirmative**	**Negative**	
Are	you				Yes, I **am**.	No, I **am not**.	
	they	going to	get	married?	Yes, they **are**.	No, they **are not**.	
Is	he				Yes, he **is**.	No, he **is not**.	

Information questions						Answers
Wh- word	*Be*	Subject	*Going to*	Verb		
What	are	you		do?		I'm going to get a job.
Where	is	she	going to	go?		To Costa Rica.
When		it		start?		In a month.

Notes
- We almost always use contractions with *be*.
- Don't use contractions in affirmative short answers. Yes, she **is**.   NOT ~~Yes, she's~~
  A: Are you **going to** go back to school?   **B:** Yes, I **am**.
- In negative answers, you can make a contraction with the pronoun and *be*. You can also make a contraction with *be* and *not*.
  A: She**'s not going to** go to the beach. Is he going to go?   **B:** No, he **isn't**.

UNIT 9, LESSON 1   PRESENT CONTINUOUS FOR THE FUTURE

When	*Be*	Subject	Verb + *ing*	Subject	*Be*	Verb + *ing*	Future time expression
	are	you		I	am		
When	is	she	leaving?	She	is	leaving	on Sunday night.
	are	we		We	are		

Notes
- We almost always contract the subject pronoun + *be* with the present continuous in speech and informal writing.
  He**'s** working in Tokyo next week.
  We**'re** taking the train to the airport.
- Use a future time expression to make the future meaning clear.
  I**'m working** on the project **next week.**
- Remember that you can also use the present continuous to talk about events happening now.
  I**'m working** on the project **now.**

IRREGULAR VERBS

Base form of verb	Simple past	Past participle	Base form of verb	Simple past	Past participle
be	was	been	leave	left	left
become	became	become	lay (off)	laid (off)	laid (off)
begin	began	begun	lose	lost	lost
break	broke	broken	make	made	made
bring	brought	brought	mean	meant	meant
build	built	built	meet	met	met
buy	bought	bought	oversleep	overslept	overslept
catch	caught	caught	pay	paid	paid
choose	chose	chosen	put	put	put
come	came	come	quit	quit	quit
cut	cut	cut	read	read	read
cost	cost	cost	ride	rode	ridden
deal	dealt	dealt	rise	rose	risen
do	did	done	run	run	run
draw	drew	drawn	say	said	said
drink	drank	drunk	see	saw	seen
drive	drove	driven	sell	sold	sold
eat	ate	eaten	send	sent	sent
fall	fell	fallen	set	set	set
feed	fed	fed	show	showed	shown
feel	felt	felt	shut	shut	shut
fight	fought	fought	sing	sang	sung
find	found	found	sit	sit	sit
fly	flew	flown	sleep	slept	slept
forget	forgot	forgotten	speak	spoke	spoken
forgive	forgave	forgiven	spend	spent	spent
freeze	froze	frozen	stand	stood	stood
get	got	gotten	steal	stole	stolen
give	gave	given	swim	swam	swum
go	went	gone	take	took	taken
grow	grew	grown	teach	taught	taught
have	had	had	tell	told	told
hear	heard	heard	think	thought	thought
hide	hid	hidden	understand	understood	understood
hit	hit	hit	wear	wore	worn
hold	held	held	win	won	won
know	knew	known	write	wrote	written

PARTICIPIAL ADJECTIVES

-ed	-ing	-ed	-ing	-ed	-ing
alarmed	alarming	disturbed	disturbing	moved	moving
amazed	amazing	embarrassed	embarrassing	paralyzed	paralyzing
amused	amusing	entertained	entertaining	pleased	pleasing
annoyed	annoying	excited	exciting	relaxed	relaxing
astonished	astonishing	exhausted	exhausting	satisfied	satisfying
bored	boring	fascinated	fascinating	shocked	shocking
charmed	charming	frightened	frightening	surprised	surprising
confused	confusing	horrified	horrifying	terrified	terrifying
depressed	depressing	inspired	inspiring	tired	tiring
disappointed	disappointing	interested	interesting	touched	touching
disgusted	disgusting	irritated	irritating	troubled	troubling

METRIC CONVERSIONS

Volume		Length and distance		Weight	
1 fluid ounce	29.57 milliliters	1 centimeter	.39 inch	1 ounce	28.35 grams
1 milliliter	.034 fluid ounce	1 inch	2.54 centimeters	1 gram	.04 ounce
1 pint	.47 liter	1 foot	.30 meter	1 pound	.45 kilogram
1 liter	2.11 pints	1 meter	3.28 feet	1 kilogram	2.2 pounds
1 quart	.95 liter	1 yard	.91 meter		
1 liter	1.06 quarts	1 meter	1.09 yards		
1 gallon	3.79 liters	1 mile	1.61 kilometers		
1 liter	.26 gallon	1 kilometer	.62 mile		

Photo Credits

Cover

Matteo Colombo/Getty Images (front), tovovan/Shutterstock (back)

Welcome Unit

Page 2: VGstockstudio/Shutterstock; 3 (front cover): Matteo Colombo/Getty Images; 4 (all images): Pearson Education, Inc.

Unit 1

Page 5: Lev Dolgachov/Alamy Stock Photo; 5 (bottom, right): Pearson Education; 6 (top right) Pearson Education; 6 (top row, online class): Rawpixel.com/Shutterstock; 6 (top row, guitar): MBI/Alamy Stock Photo; 6 (top row, japanese): LightField Studios/Shutterstock; 6 (top row, graphic design): REDPIXEL.PL/Shutterstock; 6 (top row, apartment): Goodluz/123RF; 6 (top row, job): Pixsooz/Shutterstock; 6 (bottom row, family): Oliveromg/Shutterstock; 6 (bottom row, friends): Monkey Business Images/Shutterstock; 6 (bottom row, restaurant): Wavebreak Premiumm/Shutterstock; 6 (bottom row, hospital): Dmitry Kalinovsky/123RF; 6 (bottom row, tennis): Dima Sidelnikov/Shutterstock; 6 (bottom row, chess): Sergey Nivens/123RF; 7: Pearson Education; 8 (top, right): Pearson Education; 8 (top row, lose job): Cathy Yeulet/123RF; 8 (top row, quit job): LightField Studios/Shutterstock; 8 (top row, start business): Hero Images Inc./Alamy Stock Photo; 8 (top row, engaged): Wavebreakmedia/Shutterstock; 8 (bottom row, graduate): Rawpixel/123RF; 8 (bottom row, apply to school): Rawpixel.com/Shutterstock; 8 (bottom row, change careers): Minerva Studio/Shutterstock; 8 (bottom row, nurse inset): Minerva Studio/Shutterstock; 8 (bottom row, adopt pet): Camille Tokerud/The Image Bank/Getty Images; 8 (bottom row, have baby): Ariel Skelley/DigitalVision/Getty Images; 8 (bottom row, get certificate): n_defender/Shutterstock; 9: Pearson Education; 10 (top right): Pearson Education; 10 (top row, concert): Andriy Solovyov/Shutterstock; 10 (top row, play): Kozlik/Shutterstock; 10 (top row, restaurant): Lucky Business/Shutterstock; 10 (top row, museum): Monkey Business Images/Shutterstock; 10 (bottom row, sightseeing): Rawpixel.com/Shutterstock; 10 (bottom row, shopping): altrendo images/Juice Images/Getty Images; 10 (bottom row, tour): Kzenon/123RF; 10 (icons): Andromina/Shutterstock; 11: Pearson Education; 12 (top, right): Pearson Education; 12 (left): Ferli Achirulli/123RF; 12 (center, left): Rawpixel.com/Shutterstock; 12 (center): Monkey Business Images/Shutterstock; 12 (center right, office): Cathy Yeulet/123RF; 12 (center right, construction): Dmitry Kalinovsky/Shutterstock; 12 (center right, hospital): Hxdbzxy/Shutterstock; 12 (center right, store): fiphoto/Shutterstock; 12 (right): Dragon Images/Shutterstock; 12 (bottom): Ariel Skelley/DigitalVision/Getty Images; 14 (top, right): Pearson Education; 14 (center): Songquan Deng/Shutterstock; 16 (top, right): science photo/Shutterstock; 16 (center, right): Vasyl Hubar/Shutterstock.

Unit 2

Page 17: Ammentorp Photography/Alamy Stock Photo; 17 (bottom, right): Pearson Education; 18 (top, right): Pearson Education; 18 (top row, look): Ditty_about_summer/Shutterstock; 18 (top row, feel): Constantini Michele/PhotoAlto Agency RF Collections/Getty Images; 18 (top row, smell): Ema Woo/Shutterstock; 18 (top row, taste): HBRH/Shutterstock; 18 (top row, sound): Uniquely India/Getty Images; 18 (bottom row, silk): Liliia Rudchenko/123RF; 18 (bottom row, butter): Ekaterina Markelova/Shutterstock; 18 (bottom row, coconut): Solodovnik/Shutterstock; 18 (bottom row, fire alarm): lNattapongl/Shutterstock; 18 (bottom row, movie star): Magicinfoto/Shutterstock; 19: Pearson Education; 20 (top, right): Pearson Education; 20 (top row, left): michaeljung/Shutterstock; 20 (top row, center left): YanLev/Shutterstock; 20 (top row, center): Wong yu liang /123RF; 20 (top row, center right): Wavebreak Media Ltd /123RF; 20 (bottom row, left): Cathy Yeulet/123RF; 20 (bottom row, center left): Syda Productions/Shutterstock; 20 (bottom row, center): Gorkem demir/Shutterstock; 20 (bottom row, center right): Erik Reis/123RF; 21: Pearson Education; 22 (top, right): Pearson Education; 23: Imtmphoto/123RF; 24 (top, right): Pearson Education; 24 (center, right): PR Image Factory/Shutterstock; 26 (top, right): Pearson Education; 28 (top, right): Syda Productions/Shutterstock; 28 (center, right): LStockStudio/Shutterstock.

Unit 3

Page 29: Vm/E+/Getty Images; 29 (bottom right): Pearson Education; 30 (top, right): Pearson Education; 30 (top row, exciting): Juri Pozzi/123RF; 30 (top row, excited): Muzsy/Shutterstock; 30 (top row, boring): PR Image Factory/Shutterstock; 30 (top row, bored): Marcos Mesa Sam Wordley/Shutterstock; 30 (top row, surprising): Vadim Guzhva/123RF; 30 (top row, surprised): Pathdoc/Shutterstock; 30 (bottom row, tiring): Sima/Shutterstock; 30 (bottom row, tired): Alliance/Shutterstock; 30 (bottom row, embarrassing): Stylephotographs/123RF; 30 (bottom row, embarrassed): Davidf/E+/Getty Images; 30 (bottom row, relaxing): Africa Studio/Shutterstock; 30 (bottom row, relaxed): Antonio Guillem/Shutterstock; 31: Pearson Education; 32 (top, right): Pearson Education; 33: Pearson Education; 34 (top, right): Pearson Education; 34 (top row, left): EpicStockMedia/Shutterstock; 34 (top row, center left): Syda Productions/Shutterstock; 34 (top row, center right): Federico Marsicano/Shutterstock; 34 (top row, right): Cheapbooks/Shutterstock; 34 (bottom row, left): ANURAK PONGPATIMET/Shutterstock; 34 (bottom row, center left): Iakov Filimonov/Shutterstock; 34 (bottom row, center right): Sebastian Gauert /123RF; 34 (bottom row, right): Olena Yakobchuk/

Shutterstock; 35: Sirtravelalot/Shutterstock; 36 (top, right): Pearson Education; 36 (bottom): Oliver Furrer/Alamy Stock Photo; 38 (top, right): Pearson Education; 38 (background image): Nancy Kennedy/Shutterstock; 38 (farmer's market): Arina P Habich/Shutterstock; 40: Donatas Dabravolskas/Shutterstock.

Unit 4

Page 41: Astrakan Images/ Cultura/Getty Images; 41 (bottom, right): Pearson Education; 42 (top, right): Pearson Education; 42 (salad): David Kadlec/123RF; 42 (salad dressing): Elena Veselova/123RF; 42 (wrap): My Lit'l Eye/Shutterstock; 42 (tomato soup): Martin Rettenberger/Shutterstock; 42 (pasta): Harald Walker/Alamy Stock Photo; 42 (veggie burger): Frannyanne/Shutterstock; 42 (ketchup): Macrovector/Shutterstock; 42 (cookie): NC_1/Shutterstock; 42 (fruit salad): Markus Mainka/123RF; 42 (soda): NaughtyNut/Shutterstock; 42 (iced tea): Pilipphoto/Shutterstock; 42 (lemon): Gresei/Shutterstock; 43: Pearson Education; 44 (top, right): Pearson Education; 45 (left): Chris Willson/Alamy Stock Photo; 45 (right): T-lorien/E+/Getty Images; 46 (top, right): Pearson education; 46 (top row, left): Olinchuk/Shutterstock; 46 (top row, center left): Valentina Razumova/Shutterstock; 46 (top row, center right): Pixel-Shot/Shutterstock; 46 (top row, right): Justyle/Shutterstock; 46 (center row, left): Maksim Fesenko/Shutterstock; 46 (center row, center left): Winterstorm/Shutterstock; 46 (center row, center right): Sta/Shutterstock; 46 (center row, right): Nils Z/Shutterstock; 46 (bottom row, left): Africa Studio/Shutterstock; 46 (bottom row, center): Bonchan/Shutterstock; 46 (bottom row, right): Hortimages/Shutterstock; 47: Pearson Education; 48 (top, right): Pearson Education; 48 (bottom): Kikovic/Shutterstock; 50 (top, right): Pearson Education; 50 (top): Morenovel/Shutterstock; 50 (center): Alejandro_Munoz/Shutterstock; 50 (bottom): ART Watcharapong/Shutterstock; 52: Micolas/Shuterstock.

Unit 5

Page 53: Westend61/Getty Images; 53 (bottom, right): Pearson Education; 54 (top, right): Pearson Education; 54 (top row, left): Ivan Martynyuk/Shutterstock; 54 (top row, center left): 24Novembers/Shutterstock; 54 (top row, center right): Rawpixel.com/Shutterstock; 54 (top row, right): Jakub Krechowicz/Shutterstock; 54 (bottom row, left): Rawpixel/123RF; 54 (bottom row, center left): Yentafern/Shutterstock; 54 (bottom row, center right): Suwan Waenlor/Shutterstock; 54 (bottom row, right): Rawpixel.com/Shutterstock; 55 (left): Pearson Education; 55 (right): Pearson Education; 56 (right): Pearson Education; 57 (left): Wang Tom/123RF; 57 (right): Dean Drobot/Shutterstock; 58 (top, right): Pearson Education; 58 (top row, invitation): Bloomicon/Shutterstock; 58 (top row, agenda): Kenary820/Shutterstock; 58 (top row, presentation): Andrey_Popov/Shutterstock; 58 (bottom row, video call): Rawpixel.com/Shutterstock; 58 (bottom row, refreshments): Denys Prykhodov/Shutterstock; 58 (bottom, photocopies): Chutima Chaochaiya/123RF; 58 (bottom, check equipment): Wavebreakmedia/Shutterstock; 59: Pearson Education; 60 (top, right): Pearson Education; 60 (top row, 3D): Tsz-shan Kwok/Pearson Education Asia Ltd; 60 (top row, disaster): Austinding/Shutterstock; 60 (top row, wood logs): LaMiaFotografia/Shutterstock; 60 (top row, coal): Praew stock/Shutterstock; 60 (top row, fish): Vladyslav Danilin/123RF; 60 (top row, wind turbines): T.W. van Urk/Shutterstock; 60 (top row, waste): Jim Lopes/Shutterstock; 60 (bottom row, skin): SunyawitPhoto/Shutterstock; 60 (bottom row, lungs): Magic mine/Shutterstock; 60 (bottom row, heart): Magic mine/Shutterstock; 60 (bottom row, cell): Stocktrek Images, Inc./Alamy Stock Photo; 60 (bottom): Bas Nastassia/Shutterstock; 62 (top, right): Pearson Education; 64 (top): Dreamer Company/Shutterstock; 64 (center): Who is Danny/Shutterstock.

Unit 6

Page 65: Andresr/E+/Getty Images; 65 (bottom, right) Pearson Education; 62 (top, right): Pearson Education; 66 (top row, salty): Igor Tarasyuk/123RF; 66 (top row, spicy): Mahathir Mohd Yasin/Shutterstock; 66 (top row, sweet): M. Unal Ozmen/Shutterstock; 66 (top row, bitter): Nattika/Shutterstock; 66 (top row, hot): Jreika/Shutterstock; 66 (bottom row, cold): M. Unal Ozmen/Shutterstock; 66 (bottom row, strong): John A. Anderson/Shutterstock; 66 (bottom row, weak): Anyamuse/Shutterstock; 66 (bottom row, sour): Iurii Kachkovskyi/Shutterstock; 66 (bottom row, rich): Ventura/Shutterstock; 67: Pearson Education; 68 (top, right): Pearson Education; 68 (top row, roses): Kamonrat/Shutterstock; 68 (top row, chocolates): Belchonock/123RF; 68 (top row, necklace): Shakir Pangat/Shutterstock; 68 (top row, scarf): Olga Bonchuk/123RF; 68 (top row, gift card): Charles Brutlag/Shutterstock; 68 (bottom row, card): Terry Leung/Pearson Education Asia Ltd; 68 (bottom row, tickets): Mega Pixel/Shutterstock; 68 (bottom row, perfume): Billion Photos/Shutterstock; 68 (bottom row, cologne): Garloon/123RF; 68 (bottom row, watch): Magdalena Iordache/Alamy Stock Photo; 69: Pearson Education; 70 (top, right): Pearson Education; 71: Deux/DigitalVision/Getty Images; 72 (top, right): Pearson Education; 72 (cave): Ljiljana Jankovic/Shutterstock; 72 (tiger): Aditya "Dicky" Singh/Alamy Stock Photo; 72 (polar bear): Sergei Uriadnikov/123RF; 72 (fish): Vlad61/Shutterstock; 72 (flowers): Belozorova Elena/Shutterstock; 72 (limestone): Mangojuicy/Shutterstock; 72 (cliff): Ditty_about_summer/Shutterstock; 72 (crane): Dmitry Kalinovsky/Shutterstock; 72 (platform): Benne Ochs/Getty Images; 72 (cliff): Xinhua/Alamy Stock Photo; 74 (top, right): Pearson Education; 74: Punjachoke Jittrapirom/123RF; 76 (top): Diego Cervo/Shutterstock; 76 (center): Imtmphoto/123RF.

Unit 7

Page 77: HagePhoto/Cultura RM/Alamy Stock Photo; 77 (bottom, right): Pearson Education; 78 (top, right): Pearson Education; 79 (left): Pearson Education; 79 (right): Pearson Education; 80 (top, right): Pearson Education; 80 (top row, clean): Ssguy/Shutterstock; 80 (top row, polluted): Karamysh/Shutterstock; 80 (top row, safe): Romakoma/Shutterstock; 80 (top row, unsafe): Blulz60/Shutterstock; 80 (top row, ancient): Viacheslav Lopatin/Shutterstock; 80 (top row, modern): Trabantos/Shutterstock; 80 (bottom row, famous): WDG Photo/Shutterstock; 80 (bottom row, not well known): Gerald Marella/Shutterstock; 80 (bottom row, touristy): WizData,inc./Alamy Stock Photo; 80 (bottom row, unpopular): Image Source/ DigitalVision/Getty Images; 80 (bottom row, crowded): Aleksandar Todorovic/Shutterstock; 80 (bottom row, deserted): Tororo reaction/Shutterstock; 81 (left): Pearson Education; 81 (right): Pearson Education; 82 (top, right): Pearson Education; 82 (top row, mountain): Galyna Andrushko/123RF; 82 (top row, hill): Chaivit chana/Shutterstock; 82 (top row, river): Miks Mihails Ignats/Shutterstock; 82 (top row, lake): Chon Kit Leong /123RF; 82 (top row, pond): Ramunas Miliunas/123RF; 82 (top row, ocean): Buzov Evgeny/Shutterstock; 82 (bottom row, coast): Michael Urmann/Shutterstock; 82 (bottom row, forest): Dugdax/Shutterstock; 82 (bottom row, island) Ragnar Th Sigurdsson/ARCTIC IMAGES/Alamy Stock Photo; 82 (bottom row, volcano): LukaKikina/Shutterstock; 82 (bottom row, desert): Apstockphoto/Shutterstock; 82 (bottom row, jungle): STILLFX/Shutterstock; 83: ESB Professional/Shutterstock; 84 (top, right): Pearson Education; 84 (bottom, background): Sara Winter/123RF; 86 (top, right): Pearson Education; 86 (Corona Heights): Andrew Zarivny/Shutterstock; 86 (Alcatraz): Mulevich/Shutterstock; 86 (Muir Woods): MNStudio/Shutterstock; 86 (Chinatown): R Scapinello/Shutterstock; 86 (center background): Andrew Zarivny/Shutterstock; 88 (top): Marianna Ianovska/Shutterstock; 88 (center): Galyna Andrushko/Shutterstock.

Unit 8

Page 89: PeopleImages/E+/Getty Images; 89 (bottom, right): Pearson Education; 90 (top, right): Pearson Education; 90 (top row, left): Dmytro Zinkevych/Shutterstock; 90 (top row, center left): Wavebreak Media Ltd /123RF; 90 (top row, center right): Imagenavi/Getty Images; 90 (top row, right): Jeff Morgan 01/Alamy Stock Photo; 90 (bottom row, left): Vitalii Nazarets/Shutterstock; 90 (bottom row, center left): Anita Huszti/Shutterstock; 90 (bottom row, center right): Imagenavi/Getty Images; 90 (bottom row, right): Enrique Arnaiz Lafuente/Shutterstock; 91: Pearson Education; 92 (top, right): Pearson Education; 92 (top row, left): 26kot/Shutterstock; 92 (top row, center left): John Kellerman/Alamy Stock Photo; 92 (top row center right): Christian Bertrand/Shutterstock; 92 (top row, right): Yohei Osada/ Aflo Co., Ltd. / Alamy Stock Photo; 92 (bottom row, left): KAKIMAGE2/Alamy Stock Photo; 92 (bottom row, center left): Syda Productions/Shutterstock; 92 (bottom row center right): Comstock/Stockbyte/Getty Images; 92 (bottom row, right): I store/Alamy Stock Photo; 93: Pearson Education; 94 (top, right): Pearson Education; 94 (top row, left): Rocketclips, Inc/Shutterstock; 94 (top row, center left): Maridav/Shutterstock; 94 (top row, center): Hero Images/Getty Images; 94 (top row, center right): Solis Images/Shutterstock; 94 (top row, right): ArtOfPhotos/Shutterstock; 94 (bottom row, left): Vadim Guzhva/123RF; 94 (bottom row, center left): JGI/Jamie Grill/ Blend Images/Getty Images; 94 (bottom row, center): Francesco Dibartolo/123RF; 94 (bottom row, center right): Dmitriy Shironosov/123RF; 94 (bottom row, right): AshTproductions/Shutterstock; 95: Stokkete/Shutterstock; 96 (top, right): Pearson Education; 96 (bottom, right): NeonShot/Shutterstock; 98 (top, right): Pearson Education; 98 (center): ImageSync Ltd/Alamy Stock Photo; 100 (top, right): Ucchie79/Shutterstock.

Unit 9

Page 101: Tom Merton/Caiaimage/Getty Images; 101 (bottom, right): Pearson Education; 102 (top, right): Pearson Education; 102 (left): Artazum/Shutterstock; 102 (right, top): Photographee.eu/Shutterstock; 102 (right, bottom): Akkaradet Bangchun/Shutterstock; 103: Pearson Education; 104 (top, right): Pearson Education; 104 (top row, left): dolgachov/123RF; 104 (top row, center left): Brian Overcast/Alamy Stock Photo; 104 (top row, center): Sirtravelalot/Shutterstock; 104 (top row, center right): Tommaso79/Shutterstock; 104 (top row, right):BURGER/Phanie/Alamy Stock Photo; 104 (bottom row, left): AnimalName-Design/Shutterstock; 104 (bottom row, center left): Andriy Blokhin/Shutterstock; 104 (bottom row, center): tommaso79/123RF; 104 (bottom row, center right): Pixs4u/Shutterstock; 104 (bottom row, right): VGstockstudio/Shutterstock; 104: Pearson Education; 105 (top, right): Pearson Education 107: Africa Studio/Shutterstock; 108 (top, right): Pearson Education; 108 (center left): Stanisic Vladimir/Shutterstock; 110 (top, right): Pearson Education; 110 (center) Renukayui/Shutterstock;112 (top, right): Mountaira/Shutterstock.

Unit 10

Page 113: PeopleImages/E+/Getty Images; 113 (bottom, right): Pearson Education; 114 (top, right): Pearson Education; 115: Pearson Education; 116 (top, right): Pearson Education; 116 (top row, left): Monkey Business Images/Shutterstock; 116 (top row, center left): Monkey Business Images/Shutterstock; 116 (top row, center right): Andriy Popov/123RF; 116 (top row, right): Monkey Business Images/Shutterstock; 116 (bottom row, left): WAYHOME studio/Shutterstock; 116 (bottom row, center left): Monkey Business Images/Shutterstock; 116 (bottom row, center right): Mast3r/Shutterstock; 116 (bottom row, right): Elnur/Shutterstock; 117: Pearson Education; 118 (top, right): Pearson Education; 119: Pearson Education; 120 (top, right): Pearson Education; 120 (center, right): Ariel Skelley/DigitalVision/Getty Images; 122 (top, right): Pearson Education; 123 (top, right): Rawpixel.com/Shutterstock.

Grammar Practice

Page 128 (chicken): Kpatyhka/Shutterstock; 128 (pizza): Jacek Chabraszewski/123RF; 128 (book): Bonee/Shutterstock; 128 (apples): Dionisvera/Shutterstock; 128 (tea): Melker Wickman/123RF; 128 (gum): OlegDoroshin/Shutterstock; 128 (fire alarm): Chartcameraman/Shutterstock; 128 (guitar): MillaF/Shutterstock; 133 (read newspaper): Gpointstudio/Shutterstock; 133 (start car): Pakin Songmor/123RF; 133 (lift boxes): Daxiao Productions/Shutterstock; 133 (two boys): Tatyana Tomsickova/123RF; 133 (sling): Science Photo Library/Getty Images; 133 (frustrated man): Monkey Business Images/Shutterstock; 145 (Mexico City): Ulrike Stein/Shutterstock; 145 (Warsaw): Rudi1976/123RF; 145 (Hanoi): Vietnam Stock Images/Shutterstock; 152: Kaspars Grinvalds/Shutterstock.

Illustration Credits

418 Neal (KJA Artists), John Goodwin (Eye Candy Illustration).